Differentiated Instruction in the English Classroom

CONTENT, PROCESS, PRODUCT, AND ASSESSMENT

*Barbara King-Shaver
and Alyce Hunter*

HEINEMANN
Portsmouth, NH

Heinemann

A division of Reed Elsevier Inc.

361 Hanover Street

Portsmouth, NH 03801–3912

www.heinemann.com

Offices and agents throughout the world

The authors and publisher wish to thank those who have generously given permission to reprint borrowed material:

Figures 1–1 and 4–12 are reprinted by permission from *Engaged in Learning: Teaching English, 6–12* by Kathleen and James Strickland. Copyright © 2002 by Kathleen and James Strickland. Published by Heinemann, a division of Reed Elsevier, Inc., Portsmouth, NH.

Library of Congress Cataloging-in-Publication Data

King-Shaver, Barbara.

   Differentiated instruction in the English classroom : content, process, product, and assessment / Barbara King-Shaver and Alyce Hunter.

     p. cm.

  ISBN 0-325-00577-X

   1. English language—Study and teaching (Secondary)—New Jersey—South Brunswick (Township)—Case studies. 2. Individualized instruction—New Jersey—South Brunswick (Township)—Case studies. 3. South Brunswick High School (South Brunswick, N.J.)—Case studies. I. King-Shaver, Barbara. II. Hunter, Alyce. III. Title.

  LB1631.K496 2004

  428'.0071'2—dc21   2003056576

Editor: James Strickland

Production service: Matrix Productions

Production coordinator: Sonja S. Chapman

Cover design: Jenny Jensen Greenleaf

Compositor: House of Equations, Inc.

Manufacturing: Steve Bernier

Printed in the United States of America on acid-free paper

07 06 05 04   RRD   2 3 4 5

Contents

Foreword

I t is—as it has always been—our great challenge as educators to practice our profession mired in the consuming details of the day while realizing that all we do ultimately describes not just our practices, but our beliefs. The danger is always that we become so mired in the moments of education that we lose sight of its vision.

There is no shortage, for example, of research studies reporting to us that teachers are generally aware of student differences in their classrooms, understand that those differences are significant in learning, and believe teachers teach best when they plan for instruction and instruct with student differences in mind. Those same studies, and a legion of others, report that few teachers make any substantive changes in what they teach or how they teach based on the characteristics of the individuals whom they teach.

The reasons for the disparity are many and easy to explain—at least for anyone who has spent a day with full responsibility for a room full—day full—of adolescents. There are too many kids, too many needs, too few materials, too little time, too many uncertainties about how to reach out to so many students, too few opportunities to collaborate with peers who might make our journeys both lighter and more prone to success. There are standardized tests that seem to suggest we should standardize students. There are report cards that lead us to believe we are about separating sheep from goats. And that just begins the list of justifiable reasons it is difficult to address the variance that sits before us in the classroom.

Yet there it is, nonetheless, every day. There are the students who know more than we do about what we are trying to teach. There are the students who still—in adolescence—don't know how to read at a useful level. There are students who squint at the sounds they hear while they try to learn the language of the teacher. There are students whose emotions make them threatening to the equanimity we come to value so strongly in the classroom. There are students whose cultures cause them to see the world through a lens to which our teacher-eyes have not become accustomed. There are students who hate school for any of a score of reasons. And there are so many others. As teachers, we get it that they differ in important ways. And we care to make a difference to them—at least, most of us do.

In *The Power of their Ideas*, Deborah Meier talks about what she calls "the power to care." She suggests that "powerless caring" erodes the capacity to care. Her point is that we can only care for so long if we don't know what to do to help the object of our care. Without knowing how to care, we feel helpless, hopeless—and ultimately, we have to stop caring in order to function.

That evolution from intending to care about individual students, to discouragement about teaching individuals in ways that demonstrate our caring, to resignation that attending to individual differences is infeasible happens to too many of us, I suspect. If I am correct, that is sad for the students whose educational journeys will not produce joy and power for them. And it is sad for those of us for whom the profession of teaching is less energizing and efficacious for us than it might have been—should have been.

I have enjoyed, for a variety of reasons, reading this book that Barbara King-Shaver and Alyce Hunter have written. I enjoyed it because I taught middle and high school students English for 21 years and the book feels familiar. I enjoyed it because its descriptions of classroom scenarios took me on a nostalgia trip to the days in my career when I was trying to figure out how to use time, materials, chairs, strategies, and my wits to guide a classroom in which the full range of students had a crack at genuine success. Mostly, however, I like the book because it is a tool for avoiding "powerless caring." It is an attempt to help teachers enact in the classroom the vision that propelled many of us to teaching in the first place.

I doubt that there's a teacher described in the book who'd suggest he or she has all the answers or the "right" answers for addressing student diversity. What matters is that they are developing the tools to reach out to students where they are as individuals, while still developing and teaching a "community of the whole." These are teachers who are trying to make a difference in the lives of all sorts of kids, reflecting on what works, jettisoning what doesn't, accepting the difficulty and ambiguity of it all, and still not giving up. Through this book, they show us that *how* we teach is a vehicle to demonstrate caring for both *who* we teach and *what* we teach. The book deals effectively with the daily demands on teachers and students, but does so in a way that retains the vision of a classroom as an invitational place for individuals.

I am a believer that teaching is best—for us and for our students—when it is visionary, and so there is another aspect of this book that I find intriguing. Right now, our secondary schools make clear delineations between those students whom we believe can succeed at a high level of academic expectations and those whom we believe cannot. The authors of this book argue (correctly) that within each of those demarcations is great variance needing to be addressed.

Foreword

What if we could become comfortable with attending to the inevitable variance within leveled classes? Might we then have the confidence to attend to variance in even more heterogeneous settings? Might we learn that differentiation is a means of supporting more success for more students at increasingly higher levels of expectation?

That is a vision for secondary schools that would transform the work we do and the students we teach. It could transform our country. It's worth thinking about. It's a possibility this book could help us realize.

Read the pages ahead for their practicality—and read between their lines for the possibilities they could open for us.

Carol Ann Tomlinson, Ed.D.
University of Virginia

Acknowledgments

This book would not exist without the hard work of many dedicated classroom teachers. We are thankful to members of the English Department at South Brunswick High School in New Jersey for sharing their expertise and classroom models with us, especially Patricia Abitabilo, Zandrea Eagle, Erin Farrell, April Gonzalez, Andrew Loh, Stephanie Lovero, Karen O'Holla, Lauren O'Keefe, Molly Oehrlein, and Rhonda Slawinski.

We also wish to thank math teacher Kathy Choma for sharing her classroom management strategies, AnnMarie Vanacore Remoli for adding a middle school perspective, and Kelly Maley for her expertise in teaching special education students. We are all on the same journey.

Thanks to Jim Strickland, our editor and friend, for his insistent and persistent support and to Mark Zell for his computer expertise. Finally, but never lastly, special thanks to our families, especially our spouses, Philip A. Shaver and Robert H. Hunter, for their patience and understanding.

What Is Differentiated Instruction?

Latoya sits in her ninth-grade English classroom in New Jersey, engrossed as she reads *Gone with the Wind,* picturing in her mind the world of the 1860s—the warring sides and the aftermath of the Civil War. Next to her, Stephen reads *The Watsons Go to Birmingham,* picturing in his mind the world of 1963—the interactions and changes of the Civil Rights era as seen when an African-American family from Detroit visits Alabama. Each of the readers in the classroom is guided by the same question on the board: "How does the novel you are reading depict the era it portrays?" A follow-up activity is provided, asking them to obtain a critique of the novel on-line and to read and comment on the critique.

This example provides a snapshot of differentiated instruction: A common question unites the students and their learning, although each student's choice of novel is based on his/her own readiness and interests, and a follow-up activity provides another common but differentiated anchoring experience. Still, differentiated instruction is even more than this example shows.

What is differentiated instruction? Why should middle and secondary teachers care about it? How does differentiated instruction relate to English instruction for grades 6 through 12? Does it help students score higher on high-stakes tests, such as state assessments and college entrance examinations? Will differentiated instruction help students to become better writers, readers, speakers, and listeners?

Differentiated instruction, an alternative for heterogeneous classes, addresses these questions by providing multiple avenues of learning, different challenges to different students. It asks a teacher to recognize differences and then plan and deliver accordingly, which requires extensive content knowledge as well as a vast repertoire of instructional strategies ready to match each and every student's different needs. Recognizing that one size doesn't fit all, differentiated instruction asks that each learner and his/her uniqueness be considered, embraced, and celebrated. Differentiated instruction asks teachers to diagnose students as well as analyze content and skills, to know their needs, interests, and learning styles, and to relate to students with a cognitive empathy that allows them to almost "know what's going on in each student's head."

Differentiated instruction requires flexibility and trust. The teachers try various approaches to instruction and establish flexible groups for students based on readiness, interest, and learning styles. They provide flexible time frames in which assignments can be completed, and they offer flexible lessons that allow students to reach the same goals by different paths. Teachers who embrace differentiated instruction trust themselves, and they trust their students. They trust themselves to identify the major concepts and skills students need in order to succeed, and they trust their students to make informed choices. As Strickland and Strickland (2002, 2) maintain, "We must trust our students; empower them to make decisions about their learning, to set goals, and to work at a pace that is appropriate for them."

Additionally, the concept of differentiated instruction challenges the educator to think and learn about the learning process—the "how" of learning. No one who has ever taught will deny that when students are engaged in and care about something, they will learn. As a way of thinking about teaching and learning that focuses on the individual's needs, readiness, and interests, differentiated instruction fosters objectives and activities that appeal to and engage each student. It puts the learner first and, with this primacy, directs the selection of learning objectives, activities, and assessments.

Skeptics may criticize differentiated instruction as nothing new. After all, good English teachers have been addressing individual needs and readiness for years and will continue to do so even if they have never heard the term, *differentiated instruction*, gone to any workshops, or read books on the topic. Good teachers hold individual writing conferences, modify instruction when the majority of students don't understand, individualize comments on writing assignments, and track individual growth. Yes, that is true. Good teachers have been modifying tests, lessons, and instruction and should be applauded for recognizing the need and reasons for their practice. But what is different about differentiated instruction as it is known and practiced today is that it is a deliberate and conscious method that encompasses a comprehensive way of thinking about teaching and learning. In the English classroom, it involves using specific strategies, such as developing follow-up (anchor) activities, designating alternative assignments, and choosing multiple texts. Additionally a body of knowledge is developing about differentiated instructional practices. The advice of Tomlinson (1993, 1999, 2000, 2001a), the leading authority on differentiated instruction, should be read and digested. Educators need to share what has worked and examine why, so that those at the secondary school level, who believe in this concept and its benefits, can be guided in their selection of strategies and activities that match learners' needs, interests, abilities, and prior knowledge. The purpose of this book is to begin that sharing process by providing specific answers to questions such as "How does differentiated instruction apply to middle and secondary students?" and "How can middle and secondary English teachers differentiate for 100 students a day?" This book provides definitions and examples of successful ways to differentiate, offering specific strategies and lessons.

A Primer on Differentiated Instruction

Teachers decide to differentiate their instruction based on an assessment of each individual student according to three areas of possible modification:

> Content—what a student is to learn,
> Process—how the student is to learn this content, and
> Product—how a student is to display what he/she has learned (Tomlinson 1999).

For secondary English teachers, the scope and sequence of the district and/or state curriculum and the expectations of standardized tests most often dictate content. However, because these requirements are so full of content, individual instructors, consciously or unconsciously, select what should and will be taught.

Differentiated Instruction in the English Classroom

Process is familiar to secondary English teachers. Because writing is concerned with more than a final draft, the writing is taught as an entire process: prewriting, drafting, revising, and editing. Because reading involves more than reading a text, teaching reading includes prereading strategies and postreading analysis and evaluation. Speaking and listening are language arts that are also conceived of as processes. Therefore, English teachers who are interested in differentiated instruction already believe that process is an important part of teaching and learning. Differentiated instruction challenges them to match the processes of language arts with student needs, interests, and readiness.

Product is also familiar to teachers of English. While acknowledging that process is important, teachers also accept the reality that the final product—the paper, speech, or test—ultimately shows how much a learner has achieved. However, the teachers who believe in differentiation don't feel that all learners must or should demonstrate mastery through the same written or spoken assignment. Options that match learners with products should be given. For example, one learner can write a classic five-paragraph essay and another can be challenged to compose a more complex piece. Yet another could be required to write a critique of a famous essay on the same topic that the others in the class are writing about.

In addition to content, process, and product, another possible area for modification is assessment. A teacher interested in differentiating instruction considers alternative ways to assess and evaluate the learner's product. For the same objective and the same assignment, the teacher can choose to evaluate different components. For example, suppose that two learners turn in essays about an assigned topic. A differentiating teacher might assess one paper primarily for its introduction because this essay component has been identified as one that the student needs to improve. The teacher might assess another learner primarily on the closing because this learner has struggled with creating effective closure. Another variation would be to grade each essay according to the same pre-established criteria but to give a different weight to each criterion, according to a student's needs.

A teacher determines what should be differentiated (content, process, product, and/or assessment), based on decisions about the student's readiness, interests, and learning style. A differentiating teacher uses these diagnoses to plan and implement instruction. The three areas to be considered are:

Readiness—how prepared a student is,
Interests—what a student likes, wants, and/or loves to do, and
Learning style—how a student learns best (Tomlinson 1999).

Our use of "learning style" rather than the broader category "learning profile" focuses on the environmental and neurological preferences the learner has. A more complete discussion of the "learning profile" distinctions, including the importance of gender and culture preferences, can be found in Tomlinson (1999).

Readiness

Readiness relates to both the instructional program and the learner. External instructional factors such as the expectations of the teacher, knowledge and skills of the teacher, and size of the class and its organization tangentially affect each learner's readiness. However, it is important that a teacher who wants to differentiate assess individual readiness. Physical, cognitive, social, environmental, and personal factors affect a student's readiness for certain knowledge. Specifically, teachers of English must identify deficiencies and gaps in prior knowledge and experience. For example, does a student understand definitions for literary vocabulary terms such as plot, characterization, and theme? Or does a student seem to place too much importance on personal reaction to text rather than on formal literary analysis? Conversely, teachers of English need to know which students are able to skip over an assignment to accept alternative challenges that are more in line with their readiness. For example, what can be done for a student who has moved beyond the curriculum requirement of application of literary terms to textual examples? What can be assigned to accelerate his/her learning? Should he/she be assigned the reading and writing critiques of the work being studied by the whole class? Determining individual readiness for learning is a daunting task. Traditional whole-group strategies such as pretests, surveys, and discussions can help educators discover entry points. Simple and forthright questions to help determine individual readiness—such as "What do you know about?"—can be amazingly enlightening and frightening.

Interests

What a student feels he/she wants, needs, and has to know are what capture each unique learner's curiosity, desire, and passion. Interests can be particular to a student, but they also can be age specific and/or communal. For example, one secondary English student might have a passion for *Romeo and Juliet* because he loves to write plays and wants to know more about Shakespeare's writing style. Another individual may be infatuated with *Romeo and Juliet* because she is a Leonardo DeCaprio fan and just loved him as Romeo in the contemporary film version. Additionally, most secondary students share an age-level interest in the play because the romance and family feuding portrayed captivate them. A teacher who wants to differentiate should capitalize on each and all of these students' interests. But how does a teacher discover what adolescents find of interest that might be used in English class? Specifically, how does this teacher determine what is of interest about reading, writing, speaking, and listening?

To learn about what is of interest to their students, middle and secondary English teachers can "borrow" strategies from their elementary colleagues. One strategy used to gather data on each child is called "kidwatching," in which the teacher records his/her anecdotal observations to facilitate further instruction (Owocki and Goodman 2002). Secondary and middle school teachers might likewise practice "teen watching" to determine interests and "hooks" for future learning. Although "teen watching" doesn't mean listening to and commenting during private conversations among pupils, teachers can and should learn what captivates individual students as well as what appeals to the entire class. For example, finding out about the music that the students are listening to can serve as a basic jumping-off point to begin a unit on poetry. Using what students know and are interested in will capture their attention and increase their learning. It may even let students realize that their teacher isn't so old, after all.

Another way to find out about interests is to administer interest inventory surveys. These can be general, relating to all aspects of life and learning, or specifically related to the content of the English curriculum. Teachers can generate their own questions to create a more personalized survey; one can take into account specifics such as the previous year's required reading or writing experiences that are unique to the students of a particular class or school. However it would be a mistake to include questions that address readiness on a survey gathering information about interests. A better strategy to find out about students' interests is to ask

Differentiated Instruction in the English Classroom

a reflective question, such as "What was your favorite part of the book, *To Kill a Mockingbird*? Explain why this was your favorite part." This type of query allows the learner the safety of expressing an opinion that cannot be wrong. This type of question and the subsequent answer give the teacher insight into the student as an individual and as a learner. For those who might feel insecure about generating their own interest survey, Atwell (1998) provides a sample writing and reading survey that teachers can use or modify to start the school year, giving them a way to get to know their class as readers and writers. Learners by themselves will identify areas of strength and those in need of improvement. This type of survey requires that learners take ownership of their reading and writing and be thoughtful and reflective about these processes. This type of survey reveals to the teacher not only the students' literacy skills and interests but also their ability to think about their own learning (metacognition). Burke (2000A–47) begins a survey that includes questions about frequency, enjoyment, and reading strategies, with the advice, "The more honest your answers, the better I can teach you," as a way of inviting students to act as collaborators with the teacher. This implied emphasis on collaboration reinforces one of the essential elements of differentiation: It asks the students to help the teacher know about them as persons so the information can be tailored to instruction. Strickland and Strickland (2002) provide an excellent short survey instrument that leads learners to consider how important reading is to their lives (Figure 1.1). Most importantly, when teachers employ any or all types of interest inventories or surveys to ask adolescents about themselves generally or about English learning specifically, the message to the students is, "Here is a teacher who cares about me. He/she wants to know about me! What do I like? What do I read? What don't I read? What do I write? What don't I write?"

Figure 1–1

Reading Interest Survey

1. Would you rather read a book or watch a movie?

2. What is the last book you read? Why did you read it?

3. Do you consider yourself a "reader?" How would you define that?

4. What's the best book you ever read or one of your favorites? When did you read it and why was it memorable?

5. What kinds of books do you like to read?

6. If you were to describe the place reading has in your life, how would you do so?

7. Do you ever discuss favorite books or movies with friends?

8. What would you consider a "good" book?

9. Do you ever go to libraries or bookstores?

10. Is reading important in your life? If so, how?

Reprinted from *Engaged in Learning: Teaching English, 6–12* by Kathleen Strickland and James Strickland. Copyright © 2002 by Kathleen and James Strickland. Published by Heinemann, a division of Reed Elsevier, Inc., Portsmouth, NH.

In addition to formal interest assessments, learning what students care about and want to know is as simple as asking them. A conversation or discussion with students can be illuminating not only because of their initial responses but also because of their responses to the teacher's follow-up questions. Students can be asked questions about content, process, and product and how these factors relate to their own interests. For example, a specific student who sees himself/herself as a writer might be asked how the journaling process used in the class could be made more useful. What specific type of teacher responses would help the writer become better? Such questioning helps the teacher determine ways to differentiate instruction based on interests and helps learners to become more reflective about their own reading, writing, speaking, and listening.

Learning Styles

In addition to differentiating instruction based on students' interests and readiness, teachers should also consider each student's learning style. Learning style can encompass generalities, such as intelligence preferences, gender, and culture, and specifics, such as needing to talk ideas over with peers or preferring to work alone and in writing (Tomlinson 1999, 11). To help determine students' learning profiles, teachers can use a number of published general learning style inventories. The Learning Style Inventory (LSI), popularized by Dunn and Dunn (1993), is the most comprehensive because it includes an analysis of how learners react to such diverse areas as their immediate environment, their own motivation, and physiological factors. Other learning style inventories determine whether students are auditory, visual, kinesthetic, or concrete/sequential learners based on their answers to specific questions. An example of this type of inventory is an integral part of the 4-MAT program (*The 4-MAT Coursebook* 1993). Learners answer questions to identify themselves as having one of four major learning styles. Learners include those who are interested in personal meaning, those who want to know the facts, those who are interested in how things work, and those who are involved with self-discovery. Teachers are given strategies to help each of these types of learners. Another game-type inventory, "True Colors" (Kalil, Lowry, and Berry 1999), helps learners determine their learning style by asking them to check off some of their personality traits and total point values.

Just as they did to assess students' interests, teachers can find out about their students' learning styles by observing them ("teen watching") or by asking questions. "Teen watching" for learning styles includes noticing such things as whether learners retain information better when they incorporate it into a graphic organizer or mind map or when they write it as text notes. It includes observing that some learners need to prewrite extensively in order to be organized, while others find that their ideas flow from the pen to the paper as cogent, coherent thoughts. Differentiation of instruction recognizes that each person learns differently and distinctly. It involves celebrating these differences and distinctions in the planning and implementation of instruction.

In some cases, dedicated instructors—including secondary English teachers—have used the principles and strategies of differentiated instruction for many years without naming it as such. Some teachers provide more time for some to complete tests, allow some individuals to use laptop computers while others write notes and assignments in longhand, or accommodate certain poor spellers by grading their compositions primarily on content. Some instructors adjust curriculum by pretesting and assessing what a learner already knows and altering subsequent content and activities (curriculum compacting). Others issue research assignments and learning contracts primarily on the basis of the learners' interests. Such thoughtful and caring teachers, unaware that what they have been doing and are doing is considered differentiated instruction, deliberately have chosen and continue to choose to change and modify content, process, product, or assessment to meet learners at their level of readiness, interests, and learning styles.

Middle and secondary English teachers who want to differentiate instruction in their classrooms can take heart, inspiration, and information from the successes of others, as recorded in this book, and from their own personal experiences. However hardworking and kindhearted, these teachers certainly are faced with a daunting task when they consciously and deliberately initiate and implement differentiated instruction. They are choosing to match individual students with unique levels of readiness, interests, and learning styles to altered content, process, product, or assessment. Their decision might seem like that of Prince Charming, searching for the wearer whose foot will fit the fabulous glass slipper. His search, though long and difficult, proved well worth the effort—the wonder of that just-right fit for the perfect beauty. Like Prince Charming, middle and secondary English teachers who choose to differentiate instruction are involved in a somewhat difficult process of developing their own repertoire of teaching strategies to find the wonder of that just-right fit for the perfect beauty of each of their students.

How Does Differentiated Instruction Apply to Middle and Secondary English Classrooms?

Teaching a differentiated classroom at the middle and secondary levels presents unique challenges for teachers, challenges unlike those experienced when teaching in a self-contained elementary classroom in which teachers enjoy control over the day's total schedule and have the same students all day long. As one secondary teacher commented during a workshop on differentiated instruction, "This may be fine for elementary school, but our classes are already grouped homogeneously by ability levels. Why should we be interested in differentiated instruction?"

Four Concerns about Differentiated Instruction

Middle and secondary English teachers have expressed four general concerns about the practicality and feasibility of differentiated instruction.

First, middle and high school teachers often teach classes that are grouped by ability level. Although each grade level may commonly have three levels of English—Basic Skills, Regular, and Honors—such homogeneous grouping can give the teachers and students a false sense of uniformity. Differentiated instruction teachers recognize the diversity within these ability levels. They also recognize the diversity in the field of English instruction itself. Students who are excellent writers can be grouped into a high-level class with mediocre writers who are excellent readers, and vice versa.

Second, the large numbers of students that middle and high school teachers are responsible for creates special challenges. These teachers can be responsible for teaching between 80 and 120 students or more a day, depending on the school's schedule. This is almost four times the number of students that elementary teachers teach.

Third, most secondary teachers teach more than one course. They may teach different grade levels, different courses, and/or different levels within a course. This means that teachers can have two or more courses to prepare each day. Elementary teachers are responsible for every subject during the day, but they teach them to the same students, at the same grade level. In addition, elementary teachers have the luxury of integrating language arts into the other subject areas. Middle and high school English teachers have a limited block of time in which to reach and teach classes that usually contain at least 20 students.

Fourth, many middle and high school teachers have to share classrooms and teach in more than one room during the school day. Not having their own space makes it difficult to design environments that foster cooperative work and independent learning—hallmarks of a differentiated classroom.

Despite these concerns about differentiated instruction, middle and secondary teachers can employ instructional plans and strategies to help increase learning for all their students.

Why Differentiate if the Class is Homogeneously Grouped?

The one-size-doesn't-fit-all metaphor, used frequently when presenting a rationale for differentiated instruction, applies to homogeneously grouped as well as heterogeneously grouped classes. As experienced teachers know, the ability label on any class is often misleading. It does not mean that everyone in the class is performing at the same level. Within any given class, there is always a range of ability levels. This means that when a lesson is addressed to the majority of the students, some others may need more explanation or more help and some may be bored and ready to move on. In fact some believe, "In classrooms where everyone always completes the same assignments, the teacher is probably meeting the needs of about one-fourth of the students" (Wormeli 2001, 72). As discussed previously, differentiating instruction is not based solely on ability levels or readiness; lessons can be differentiated according to student readiness, interests, and learning styles. Even in a class as homogeneously grouped academically as Advanced Placement (AP) English, differences exist in the students' interests and learning styles.

Whether classes are homogeneously grouped or heterogeneously grouped by ability levels, some students have more expertise than others, based on their skills or prior knowledge for any given unit within any given course. For example, a student who has seen a performance of *Romeo and Juliet* may be better able to read and understand the text on his or her own than a student who has never seen or read a Shakespearean play before. For this reason, lessons must be adjusted for interests and learning styles as well as for academic readiness.

How Can Middle and Secondary English Teachers Differentiate for 100 Students a Day?

The easy answer to the question of how teachers differentiate for 100 students a day is: They don't. Teachers who teach multiple classes of 20 or more students usually do not differentiate in every class for every unit. They do not need to plan differentiated lessons daily. When teachers, regardless of grade level, decide to differentiate, they are advised to start small so that differentiating does not overwhelm either them or the students (Wehrmann 2000). This is especially true for middle and secondary classroom teachers who teach multiple classes. Starting small may be as simple as differentiating homework assignments or adding choice into reading and writing assignments.

When differentiating homework, teachers must consider the full range of readiness in their classes—those more advanced as well as those who need additional help. They must identify the purpose of a homework assignment to look for ways to alter the assignment so that the students are all working toward the same goal. For example, if students are studying vocabulary connected to a text they are reading, the majority of the class may be asked to complete a traditional vocabulary homework assignment, one asking them to define the words and write sentences showing that they know the meaning of the words as they are used in the text. For less proficient students, the list may be shortened to key words, those needed for comprehension. Advanced students may be asked to find alternative definitions for the words, or they could be asked to supply synonyms for the assigned words and then to distinguish differences in connotation between the original word and its synonym. The advanced students are not being asked to do more work but to do a different type of work, work that is more suited to their ability level.

Middle and secondary teachers who carry a large roster of students also find it helpful to begin differentiating with one lesson that is part of a core unit in one class. This is especially helpful for teachers who are new to differentiated instruction. They find it easier to limit the ways they differentiate. They may choose to differentiate the content, process, or product based on interest, readiness, or learning styles. Teachers do not have to address multiple forms of differentiation, such as varying content and process, until they are more comfortable with the process of differentiating lessons. For example, when studying *The Diary of a Young Girl* by Anne Frank, all learners can be required to complete a research report. All can be required to use the same research process. All can be required to produce the same product—a written report. Topics for the research, however, could be suggested based on student interests. These could include such diverse subjects as art and music created in concentration camps or the history of the theatrical production of *The Diary of a Young Girl*.

After teachers have planned several differentiated lessons, they can advance to planning a core unit that incorporates activities addressing student differences. They can then present the unit of study to one class and monitor how well it succeeds. At the end of the unit, they should reflect on the content, process, and product and make revisions as needed before teaching the same unit to another class. Following this procedure, a teacher may have differentiated only two or three new units in a school year. By focusing on a few units, the teacher can take the time to assess the students' needs and to plan differentiated lessons accordingly.

In addition, teachers may choose to work with colleagues to develop multiple units. A teacher works on a unit plan, receives peer feedback from a colleague, teaches the unit, and reflects on it.

This teacher then shares the completed unit plan with his/her colleague and vice versa. This yields a two-for-one model of unit development. Using this model, each teacher receives differentiated plans for two different units. Even though each class is unique and the unit plans will have to be adapted to fit their particular students, the two teachers will not have to begin from scratch when developing each lesson plan that incorporates differentiated lessons. Examples of such plans are presented in Chapter 6.

Another approach is for teachers to develop generic activities that support differentiation. These activities can then be introduced into any unit. For example, a generic differentiated activity might be building student choice into reading and writing assignments, a practice familiar to many teachers. After teachers have identified the need to differentiate for a student, or group of students, within a unit of study, they can incorporate some of the generic strategies developed and adapt them as needed. Some generic strategies are described with examples in Chapter 5.

When beginning to differentiate any unit or lesson, teachers must consider not only the *what* but also the *why*. Differentiation requires that teachers clarify their own thinking in relation to the specifics of English instruction. What should all learners in English know and be able to do? What should students who meet these goals and objectives be challenged to do? How can each learner be helped and accommodated? All assignments should begin with clear goals and objectives. When teachers are clear about where their students are going, they can plan various ways for the students to get there.

How Do Teachers Who Share Rooms Create an Environment for Differentiated Instruction?

One of the challenges unique to middle and secondary teachers is creating environments that support flexible grouping. Often

Differentiated Instruction in the English Classroom

middle and secondary teachers have to share classrooms and/or move from room to room each day. This creates the challenge of reorganizing the seating arrangements in classrooms whenever the teacher wants to differentiate by having the students participate in group work or independent study. In addition, most secondary classrooms are equipped with individual desks that have attached chairs. These student desks are frequently placed in rows facing the front of the room.

Seating Supports Differentiation.   Kathy Choma, a math teacher at South Brunswick High School in New Jersey, has devised a system for seating that supports differentiated instruction. Her seating arrangement is based on student readiness and allows for flexible grouping. In Choma's model, her seating arrangement has rows of students who can work independently and learn new concepts quickly seated adjacent to rows of students who need more time and practice to learn new concepts. For example, students who are more advanced form row A; students who need more help form row B; students who are advanced form Row C; students who need more help form row D, and so on. The rows alternate by readiness level. This allows for different forms of flexible grouping by ability levels. When the teacher wants the students to work together in same-ability groups, the students form a group by working with others in their row. When a teacher such as Choma wants students to work in mixed-ability groups, the students form groups by working with their four corners. For example, the two students who are first in rows A and B meet with those who are second in rows A and B (see Figure 2.1a). Additionally, for partner work such as think-pair-share, students may work with the person next to them (mixed ability) or the person seated in front or behind them (same ability, see Figure 2.1b).

Figure 2–1a Mixed-Ability Groups

Row A	Row B		Row C		Row D
x	x		x		x
x	x		x		x
x	x		x		x
x	x		x		x

Mixed Ability Level Group   Same Ability Level Group

Figure 2–1b Same-Ability And Mixed-Ability Partner Work

Row A	Row B	Row C	Row D
x	x	x	x
x	x	x	x
x	x	x	x
x	x	x	x
x	x	x	x
x	x	x	x

Same Ability   Mixed Ability
Level Partners   Level Partners

Arranging the class this way helps students move into pairs and small groups with ease. During the school year, rows can be changed based on student progress and topics being studied. A student who is in a high-ability row for one topic may be in another row for a different topic. Choma does not share the levels of the rows with the students, and, because she uses a variety of groups among the rows during a unit, the purpose of the seating arrangements is not readily recognized. It also allows the teacher to place students closer to the front if they need to see or hear better, or need special coaching, such as non-native English speakers.

This type of seating arrangement also makes it easier for the teacher to work with those students who need additional instruction or tutoring while providing opportunities for students who can work independently to apply what they have learned in new ways. Choma's seating arrangement works well when lessons are differentiated according to student readiness. When lessons are differentiated based on student interest or learning style, another seating arrangement may be needed.

Ann Marie Vannacore, a former eighth-grade language arts teacher, turned over responsibility for the arrangement of space to each of her five classes. She divided each class into cooperative groups, charging each group to plan a room arrangement that would most benefit instruction, specifically differentiated teaching and learning. Each group had to create a diagram of the physical layout of the room and then present its diagram and a written rationale for it to the whole class. Ann Marie gave the students parameters for the arrangement: it must be completed in two minutes; it must recognize that other teachers and classes use the room; and the majority of class time must be spent in learning, not in moving furniture. After the groups presented their proposals, the class voted, selecting the arrangement they felt was best for their class to use when the time came for differentiating lessons. The teacher posted each class's plan in the room, abiding by the plans for the rest of the year. Not only did these eighth graders feel they had control and ownership of their classroom but also they learned the essential language of persuasive writing and speaking.

Resources Support Differentiation. In addition to organizing the seating arrangement and groups in a classroom, teachers who address learning differences in their classes also have materials ready for lessons that support different learning styles and multiple readinesses. For example, these teachers carefully organize the resources in their rooms such as classroom libraries, art supplies, tape recorders, and CD players. If possible, they provide computers and printers. Teachers who are fortunate enough to have their own classrooms create learning areas that support sustained silent reading, project work, and technology.

How Well Does Differentiated Instruction Fit an English Class?

Differentiated instruction is a natural fit for English classes. English teachers are already using many of the teaching and learning strategies that support differentiated instruction. The inclusion of student choice in assignments, such as outside readings and essay topics, supports student differences in readiness and interests. Having small groups of students discuss different texts in literature circles addresses both student interest and readiness in the English class. In addition, English teachers often employ performance assessments with units of study that include multimodal products. Performance assessments frequently ask students to investigate a topic, such as Elizabethan England, and present what they have learned in both oral and written forms. The oral presentation may also have visuals accompanying it.

Writing workshop, another practice widely used in many English classes, can be seen as a microcosm of a differentiated class. In a writing workshop, students select their own topics based on personal interests and prior experiences. The students work alone, with a partner, or in small groups writing, revising and editing their papers during different stages of the writing process. Within any given writing class, student writers who need different amounts and types of help from the teacher receive minilessons and participate in one-on-one conferences. In addition, a writing workshop offers students the opportunity to work at their own pace. What does not vary in the writer's workshop is the goal: every student is responsible for completing the writing process and submitting a final paper. The practices that make writing workshops a success are same elements found in differentiated classrooms. The difference between using these strategies in a traditional classroom or in a differentiated instruction classroom is that in the differentiated classroom, student differences and needs are clearly identified and lessons are planned based on individual readiness, interests, and learning styles.

What Does a Differentiated Classroom Look Like?

Although no one would claim that differentiated classrooms look alike, certain principles help to identify a differentiated classroom (Tomlinson 1999). These include:

- All students participate in respectful work.
- Flexibility is evident in all aspects—from grouping to tasks.
- Assessment and instruction are connected and intertwined.

Still, the distinction between a differentiated class and a traditional class may not be readily apparent. In fact, one might need to observe a class over time to determine whether it exemplifies differentiated instruction. Most notably, one might look for the variety of ways groups of students and individuals are configured within the same classroom. The majority of students may be seen working in small groups, while other students are working individually at their seats and still others are meeting with the teacher. In addition, some students may be reading while others are drawing and still others are using a computer. Differentiated English classes are fluid and use a variety of personalized "maxi" and "mini" strategies to study the same core objectives. Students are actively constructing knowledge as they consciously, with more or less teacher direction, move literally and figuratively between group and individual experiences.

Additional evidence of differentiated instruction might be revealed by visiting a classroom over time:

- teachers beginning where students are;
- teachers engaging students through different learning modalities;
- students competing more against themselves than others;
- teachers providing specific ways for each individual to learn;
- teachers using classroom time flexibly; and
- teachers acting as diagnosticians who prescribe the best possible instruction for each student (Tomlinson 1999).

All of these characteristics could not be readily observed in a one-time visit, yet they are an integral part of the ongoing teaching and learning process.

With flexibility as the guiding differentiating principle, a middle or secondary teacher of English would employ different groupings, assignments, time frames, and assessments. Differences would be determined based on an analysis of each individual student. Flexible grouping begins with an understanding that students work and learn best in a variety of classroom configurations. Figure 3.1 explains one possible pattern for such flexible grouping. In this figure, the four scenarios indicate the main ways teachers group students in their classes: whole class, individuals, pairs, and small groups. In a differentiated classroom, variations within groupings

Differentiated Instruction in the English Classroom

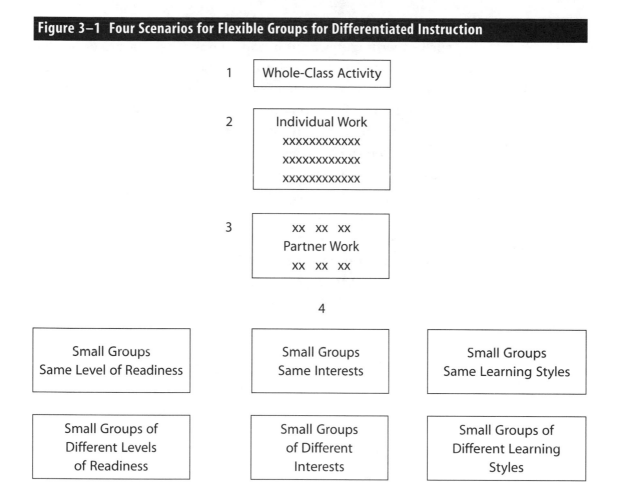

allow for differences in content, process, and product based on student readiness, interests, and learning styles, as shown in the variations within scenario 4 in Figure 3.1.

In a differentiated classroom, students may move between the various configurations during different lessons or units of study. The decision for students to work independently, in small groups, or as a whole class is more commonly determined by the teacher, but it can also be based on student choice. For example, the

What Does a Differentiated Classroom Look Like?

teacher may introduce a concept in a unit to the whole class, such as writing powerful introductions. Then, based on a pre-assessment of student writing ability and familiarity with this particular concept, the teacher may assign students to specific small groups to work, based on their readiness. Within the same lesson, one or two students may be ready to move beyond the planned lesson, as indicated by their previous performances. For example, the advanced students might be ready to try writing more sophisticated openings for their papers. These students could be given an alternative assignment and be working independently during the same class. Thus, while students in the small groups are analyzing the openings of essays in *Time* or *Newsweek*, the two advanced students could be reading independently to find examples of powerful openings in *The New Yorker* or *Atlantic Monthly*.

At times, students may self-select to work independently or in small groups, based on interests or learning styles. One example of this can be seen when the teacher offers choices of the products to be presented by the students. As part of a unit on *A Separate Peace*, for example, students may be given the assignment to present a character analysis of Finny or Gene in any mode they choose. To complete this assignment, they are given the options of electing to work alone, with a partner, or in a small group. They can also decide whether they wish to present their character analysis in the form of a written paper, a visual presentation, or a creative dramatic or musical presentation.

Groups do not have to remain intact for an entire unit of study, but can be rearranged for different tasks. A student who is weak in one area may be strong in another; therefore, the teacher can place him or her in different groups during the same unit of study because a unit comprises a number of lessons and activities. For example, during a poetry unit, a student who may be good at understanding the message of poems may have difficulty identifying and explaining the literary devices used to create the meaning. The teacher could place this student, based on previous performance, in an advanced group during the reading of a poem and the discussion of its meaning and then move that student into a second group for an analysis of the literary devices employed by the poet. Flexible grouping eliminates the labeling of any one group as "high" or "low," which can be damaging in middle and secondary classrooms where students are very attuned to public labels. Grouping students for learning in this flexible way demonstrates some of the essential characteristics of differentiated instruction. It allows teachers and students to create a student-centered classroom built upon trusting relationships and fluid activities.

Another challenge for the English classroom teacher is the movement toward more heterogeneously grouped classes. Many school districts are eliminating multilevel courses and separate classes for special populations, such as gifted and talented students and special education students.

How Does Differentiated Instruction Work in an Inclusion English Classroom?

One way in which English classes are becoming less homogeneous is the inclusion of special education students, which results in students with special needs working side by side with the general student population. What used to be called "mainstreaming" is now more commonly referred to as "inclusion"; that is, students who used to be taught in self-contained special education classrooms are now being placed in regularly scheduled classes. In an inclusion classroom, learners with special needs are "included" with the general population. These learners represent a wide array of special needs, including learning disabilities, communication disorders, attention deficit disorders, physical impairments, and social and emotional disorders. Teachers with special needs students in their classes must consult the students' individualized educational plan (IEP) or a representative of the child-study team to determine what, if any, modifications to the learning program need to be made for the inclusion students. The child-study team in a school consists typically of a learning specialist, a school psychologist, a social worker, and a special education supervisor or teacher.

The number and roles of the adults in the classroom define different inclusion models. In one model, the special needs student is placed in a regularly scheduled English class, and the English teacher, as the only adult in the room, is responsible for the planning and delivery of instruction and the assessment of learning. In a second model, a paraprofessional or classroom aide assists the English teacher. In a third model, two licensed teachers co-teach. In coteaching, the two teachers, an English teacher and a special education teacher, share all aspects of instruction and have joint responsibility for the class.

Although the inclusion classroom provides a unique opportunity for using various forms of differentiated instruction, the danger is that all special education students will be grouped together, forming a class within a class. At times the special education teacher may work with a small group of special needs students, but these periods of direct instruction should not last very long. The grouping of the special needs students for instruction should be just one of the many groupings that are formed during a unit of study. When groups are formed based on readiness, interests, and learning styles, the special needs student will have many opportunities to work with a variety of others in the class.

If implemented correctly, the co-teaching model can benefit all students in the class because two professionals are cooperatively planning lessons, delivering instruction, and assessing student work. Although the English teacher may have more content area knowledge, the special education teacher may be more knowledgeable about strategies that help all learners, particularly struggling students.

The special education teacher, furthermore, is often an excellent resource for learning how to modify and differentiate instruction. By choice and training, special education professionals have learned ways to adapt and alter instruction to accommodate student needs, interests, and learning profiles. These professionals are also frequently skilled in how to teach test-taking strategies and how to alter product and assessment. For example, special educators suggest differentiated strategies such as asking learners (either in writing or orally) why they chose a particular answer for a multiple-choice test and then why they did not choose the other answers. When teachers try new ways to look at the learning and thought processes of their students, such as this type of comprehensive assessment strategy, all learners can benefit from the improved self-reflection activity.

How Does Differentiated Instruction Work in a Class with Gifted and Talented Students?

Differentiated instruction reminds many people of the gifted and talented programs that have been so controversial for many years in this country. Parents, teachers, and administrators have had difficulty agreeing what constitutes "gifted and talented," who the gifted and talented students might be, and what programs are best for them. In some schools gifted and talented programs are based on academic performance, and others emphasize areas such as art or music. Some gifted and talented programs have been based on a pull-out system in which the students are removed from their regular classes for a limited amount of time to receive special instruction or participate in enrichment activities. Other programs have placed gifted and talented students together in self-contained classes. As a result of these disagreements over which programs best meet student needs, and in light of budget restraints, many self-contained gifted and talented classes are being eliminated, returning the gifted and talented students to regular classes. This increases the ability range of students an English teacher needs to address within one class. Gifted and talented students may have special gifts, but they also have special learning needs.

In fact, "differentiated learning for high-ability students in heterogeneous classrooms is as important as it is for other children, yet the needs of the gifted are often misunderstood" (Winebrenner 2001, 52). Despite the fact that these high-ability students can reach the state standards with ease, they need work that is more challenging in complexity and depth.

Some middle and secondary English teachers may argue that the gifted and talented students are homogeneously grouped in honors classes and, therefore, do not need differentiated instruction. Experience has shown that even within honors classes, there is a range of abilities for various academic and political reasons. Some students may be taking the honors class to challenge themselves; some parents may have waived the prerequisites for honors and placed their children in the class; and some students may be gifted in one area of English study but not in another. For example, a student who excels at poetry may not necessarily excel when writing a persuasive essay. Although the range and frequency of differentiated instruction in honors classes may not be as great as in regular English classes, there are still times when some students in these classes would benefit from differentiated lessons.

Curriculum Compacting

Academically advanced students are prime candidates for differentiated instruction in the form of curriculum compacting, a strategy that allows students to be accelerated based on readiness. This form of differentiated instruction gives them a chance to demonstrate mastery of content and then move beyond the basic curriculum. The areas these students have mastered are identified by a preassessment, which the teacher uses as an indication of how to develop lessons that address the same goals as the whole class yet challenge the academically advanced student. The teacher must be careful to plan activities that are qualitatively, not quantitatively, different from the whole-class activities. For example, in a poetry unit, the students who excel in reading and analyzing poetry should not be given more poems to read but should be asked to analyze poems that are cognitively more demanding. For example, if tenth graders are analyzing the form and imagery of the two "caged bird" poems, "Sympathy" by Paul Laurence Dunbar and "Caged Bird" by Maya Angelou, the high-ability students might be asked to analyze form and imagery in "The Caged Skylark" by Alexander Pope. After each group has finished its analysis, the class could meet as a whole to compare the findings. Bringing the groups of students together for a sharing of their analyses would be a rich learning experience for the whole class. The point is not to give these advanced students more work, but to give them work that is more complex or abstract, asking them to work at the higher levels of Bloom's taxonomy (1956).

Just as the grading procedure for the whole class shouldn't be based solely on the mastery of content but on preparation, participation, and productivity, students doing compacting should be graded the same way. Compacting requires that teachers give students credit for having mastered the course content but consider these other elements as well.

Extension Activities

In addition to knowing material before it is formally taught, gifted and talented students often work at an accelerated pace (Winebrenner 2000). Even when the material is new, higher-level students may be able to work faster than the majority of students in their class. When they do so, the teacher can have extension activities prepared for them to do. Extension activities in English can include independent reading of more complex texts, independent research into a topic, creative writing projects, and studying literary theories.

How Do Teachers Grade in a Differentiated English Classroom?

There is controversy among proponents of differentiated instruction as to how to grade work when students in the same class are working at different levels of complexity. Teachers must remember that "the purpose of grading is to give students (and their parents) feedback about their learning progress and the quality of their work"; therefore, teachers should grade student work based on "the degree to which their performance reflects [the teacher's] criteria for good work" (Heacox 2002, 119). The controversy in this philosophy is that students are working on different sets of criteria depending on which assignment they are doing. A teacher who creates assignments that reflect different degrees of academic challenge establishes clear evaluation criteria for each specific assignment. However, not all students do the same assignments.

In a classroom in which differentiated instruction is used, students may be working on different tasks and, therefore, have different sets of criteria to meet. Proponents of differentiated instruction argue that this practice is fair because each student is working to the best of his/her ability and moving ahead on the learning continuum.

Ideally, assignments in a differentiated classroom are evaluated according to whether they meet the criteria for that particular task. Additionally, the teacher does not have to be the only one in the room assessing student work. When the criteria for an assignment are given to the students, they are able to self-assess or peer-assess. This is frequently done in English classes for writing assignments but can also be used effectively for oral presentations and group work.

The issue of grading becomes more complex when assessing students who have compacted out of doing the required core content. Should those students be graded based on the extension work they complete beyond the core, or should they be given full credit for having mastered the core content already? Winebrenner (2001) believes that students who compact out of an area of study should be given full credit for the mastery they have demonstrated. Thus, when these students complete extension activities, they should be given feedback but not grades for their work. Some wonder why, then, would these students be willing to do the extension work. Educators who have studied gifted and talented students have found that these students enjoy a challenge and dislike being bored in class. They have noted that students who complete challenging extension activities appreciate the recognition of their talents and the feedback they receive.

Some parents and teachers, however, believe that students working on extension activities will not complete these assignments carefully if they know their work will not be graded but simply be assessed.

Because of the many issues associated with grading in a differentiated classroom, it is important that teachers:

- Know their district's policy

- Communicate their grading system to the parents early in the school year, explaining not just how grades are determined, but also why the system is this way
- Give criteria to individual students when a task is assigned so that they know what is expected for a top performance.

Many teachers find that distributing a rubric for an assignment (such as those shown in Chapter 6) helps students and parents understand exactly what the criteria for an assignment are and how the work will be assessed.

How Does Differentiated Instruction Affect Preparing Students for High-Stakes Tests?

When English teachers are invited to try differentiated instruction in their classrooms, a common reaction is, "Differentiating instruction sounds great; who doesn't want to reach all students and have them learn? But if my students don't score well on those tests, the parents and the principal will be angry! Newspaper articles don't care if my students and I differentiate. They only report the test scores, and if they are bad, I look bad and so does my school." Such reactions seem to indicate that differentiation of instruction and high-stakes testing are perceived to be at the very least incompatible and possibly even antagonistic with each other. However, this is simply not true.

Differentiated instruction is not in conflict with high stakes testing. Differentiated instruction does not mean that there are different goals for each student. Rather it demands that teachers identify essential goals for all. Because good teachers are concerned about their students' success on high-stakes tests, these essentials should not be generated in a vacuum but be determined after consulting state and national goals, objectives, and testing formats. Teachers who differentiate offer a variety of ways for students to achieve the essential goals and outcomes. For example, if a teacher knows that the state test requires learners to produce an expository composition based on a cause/effect prompt that will be scored using a rubric, the teacher as diagnostician will first determine the students' levels of readiness: "Has the student ever written an expository composition? Does he/she know the difference between cause and effect?" The teacher also finds out about the students' writing histories and their interests in specific topics. The teacher, mindful of the common goal, will use this information to make decisions about how and what to teach each student, calling upon a wide range of instructional strategies needed to accomplish this individualization and differentiation. For some, concentration is on writing effective transitions between thoughts, sentences, and paragraphs. For others, work has to be done to help them understand the difference between cause and effect. Others might need to concentrate on sentence structure and spelling.

Differentiated instruction has the potential to reach each and all of these learners. It should focus teaching and learning around commonly accepted and tested goals and objectives—the requirements of high-stakes testing. In addition, differentiated instruction has the power to unite levels of readiness, interests, and learning profiles with appropriate yet individualized and differentiated content, process, product, and/or assessment to foster student success on these goals, these tests, and in all learning.

How Do Teachers Manage a Differentiated Classroom?

Teachers plan for differentiation of instruction by learning about their students personally and academically. Ascertaining personal information about students' likes, dislikes, hobbies, and activities helps teachers when planning lessons that are differentiated based on student interests. Similarly, assessing a student's prior knowledge and learning preferences helps teachers when planning lessons that are differentiated based on readiness or learning styles.

Preassessment for interests is done frequently at the beginning of the school year. Teachers can identify areas of student interests and expertise, and they can build on these interests when planning learning experiences. For example, if a student is involved in competitive skateboarding, the teacher may collect titles of magazines and books that address this topic.

It may take time to obtain information on student readiness, interests, and learning styles at the beginning of a school year or a new unit, but it is time well spent when the goal is helping all students learn to the best of their ability. Taking the time to find out what students know, what their interests are, and what their learning styles are helps teachers know their students better both academically and personally. These activities benefit both the students and the teacher.

Getting to Know Students: Their Interests

One way for teachers to get to know their students' interests better is to use ice-breaking activities. These activities have been tried with students from elementary school through graduate school, and students consistently respond positively to them.

For example, "Find-Someone-Who" is a strategy that asks students to get up and mix with their classmates to find someone who has the interests described on a prepared interest sheet (Kagan 2000). At the end of the activity, the teacher can collect the sheets and read them in order to learn more about the students' interests. Figure 4.1 shows an adaptation of this activity: Getting-to-Know-Me.

Another icebreaker combines personal and academic information: Getting-to-Know-You Vocabulary Icebreaker (Figure 4.2). The teacher prepares this sheet ahead of time by listing Scholastic Aptitude Test (SAT) vocabulary words on a prepared sheet and asking the students to introduce themselves by identifying which words describe their likes and their dislikes. The students use these statements to introduce themselves to the whole class. The teacher can collect all sheets and review them to learn more about his/her students.

Interest inventories, as we suggested earlier, are an additional way to obtain the likes and dislikes of students. Many published interests surveys are available, or a teacher may create her own, such as the one presented in Figure 4.1. Additionally, visual learners may

Differentiated Instruction in the English Classroom

Figure 4–1

Getting to Know Me

Name _____ Nickname _____

1. My three favorite pastimes are

   _____ _____ _____

2. My pet peeve is _____

3. The best book I ever read was _____

4. The music I prefer to listen to is _____

5. My favorite subject is _____

6. The subject I struggle with the most is _____

7. One goal I have is to _____

8. As a student, I _____

9. The best movie I ever saw was _____

10. In the summer you would most likely find me _____

prefer to represent their interests by creating a collage or by bringing a favorite item to class and explaining its significance to them. For students who prefer writing, a journal entry can provide an open-ended way for students to introduce themselves. Another way to learn more about students is to have them interview each other and then introduce their partners to the whole class, stressing their partner's likes and dislikes.

How Do Teachers Manage a Differentiated Classroom? • **43**

Figure 4–2

Getting-to-Know-You Vocabulary Icebreaker

Name _____ Date _____

PART ONE

Read over the following list of words and choose two that describe you and two that do not describe you. Explain how each word does or does not pertain to you. The brief explanation must show that you know the meaning of the word.

For example:

> I am very *gregarious*. I can start a conversation with complete strangers while waiting in line to buy groceries.

> I am not *lackadaisical*. If anything, I work too hard.

You will be introducing yourself to the whole class using two of the four words you selected. By the end of the week, everyone will be responsible for knowing all of the words listed here.

diffident	intransigent	munificent
judicious	insouciant	circumspect
petulant	belligerent	perspicacious
lugubrious	impervious	intrepid
tenacious	supercilious	laconic
sagacious	altruistic	indigent
dejected	demure	ebullient
impecunious	unassuming	benevolent
insolent	discreet	fastidious
decorous	ingenuous	

PART TWO

Complete the following sentences with information that describes you. You are also responsible for knowing the italicized words.

I have a *propensity* toward _____

I have an *affinity* for _____

I have an *antipathy* to _____

I have been known to be *remiss* in _____

Getting to Know Students: Their Readiness

Teachers should also obtain information on the students' academic readiness when beginning a new unit of study. Consider how often a topic, including a work of literature, is taught as if everyone in the class knew nothing about it. For example, consider how many times Shakespeare's life and the Globe Theater are taught in English classes between grades 6 and 12. It is no wonder that students roll their eyes when a senior English teacher begins to draw a diagram of the Globe Theater on the chalkboard. If there are 25 students in a class, there are 25 people with different prior knowledge. It is important to find out what that knowledge is. When this is obtained, teachers can plan lessons that build on that knowledge and differentiate lessons as needed. English teachers can ascertain readiness in general areas such as writing and reading early in the school year. An effective way to identify student differences in writing is to obtain a writing sample at the beginning of the school year. This may be a timed writing on an assigned writing topic or a piece of writing completed outside class. One advantage of a timed writing topic is that students have the same writing topic and the same time frame for writing. Another advantage of a timed writing sample is that the teacher knows that the student alone is solely responsible for the writing. The disadvantage is that a timed sample may not represent a student's best work. A learner may not know anything about a particular topic or be able to relate to it and therefore find it difficult to write about. Teachers can begin the process of differentiation by providing a variety of topics for these timed writings. Some teachers, to obtain a more comprehensive view of a learner, collect both types of writing at the beginning of the year. The writing topic might commonly be connected to a book read over the summer.

Obtaining evidence of differences in reading ability early in the school year is not as easy as it is for writing. One way to obtain this information is to check the students' scores on a recent standardized test, but the information included there may be outdated or inaccurate, based as it is on a one-time snapshot of the students' performance. Students can self-report their past experiences as readers (see Figure 4.3). This is, by nature, subjective, but it provides insights into how students see themselves as readers. Even if it is not academically accurate, it provides a good starting point.

Two effective prereading strategies for assessing prior knowledge involve using a KWL chart (Ogle 1986) and a Prereading List. On a KWL chart, the first two of three columns are completed before reading about or studying a given topic. In the first column, students identify what they know about a certain topic (K). In the second column, they brainstorm what they want to know about the topic (W). After reading or studying the topic, students return to the KWL chart and complete the third column, what they learned (L). Figure 4.4 presents a sample K-W-L chart for students' pre- and poststudy of *The Great Gatsby*.

A Prereading List is a similar strategy that can also be used with any genre (Figures 4.5, 4.6, and 4.7). The students are given a list of terms and asked to identify those they know well enough to teach, those they know fairly well, those they have heard of but are not quite sure of, and those that are unknown to them. Reviewing the students' responses to this list can help teachers decide whether some students are already familiar with the material to be studied. Differentiated lessons and assignments can then be made based on the information obtained.

Getting to Know Students: Their Learning Styles

"Learning style is a gestalt that tells us *how* a student learns and prefers to learn" (Keefe and Jenkins 2002, 443). Knowing their students' learning styles helps teachers plan instruction and assessment that are meaningful to each individual.

Differentiated Instruction in the English Classroom

Figure 4–3

English Survey

Name _____ Date _____

1. My favorite author is _____.

2. The best book I ever read was _____.

3. *Please circle as many as apply to you:*
   When I have to write an essay, I

   put it off until the last minute.   write it as fast as I can.

   get help revising and editing.   take time to plan it out.

4. *Please circle as many as apply to you:*
   When I am reading, I

   need it quiet around me.   predict what comes next.

   stop and reread many times.   give up when it is too difficult.

5. I prefer to read (circle as many as apply to you)

   novels   short stories   plays   poetry.

6. When I am asked to read aloud I am (circle one)

   confident   embarassed   angry

7. If given free choice, I would like to write about _____

   _____ .

8. If given free choice, I would like to read about _____

   _____ .

9. One goal I have is to _____

   _____ .

10. As a student, I _____

    _____ .

11. The best movie I ever saw was _____

    _____ .

12. In the summer you would most likely find me _____

    _____

    _____ .

How Do Teachers Manage a Differentiated Classroom?   • **47**

Figure 4–4

Sample KWL Chart for *The Great Gatsby* by F. Scott Fitzgerald

Student's Name _____   Unit/Text *The Great Gatsby* by F. Scott Fitzgerald

What I Know (About the 1920s)	**What I Want to Know** (About the 1920s)	**What I Learned** (About the 1920s)
The Roaring Twenties were wild	Was everybody partying?	Music was important.
People danced the jitterbug.	Was it the same everywhere?	People danced the Charleston.
There were speakeasies.	Why did it end?	The Depression started.
	Who were the famous people?	Not everyone was partying.
	What else did Fitzgerald write?	Fitzgerald was a spokesperson for his generation.
		Fitzgerald wrote *This Side of Paradise* as a young man.
		Fitzgerald captured the American Dream—its good and bad points.

Figure 4–5

Name _____ Date _____

Prereading List for *The Scarlet Letter*

Place a "T" next to the terms you know well enough to teach to someone else.

Place an "H" next to the terms you have heard of.

Place a question mark "?" next to terms that are new to you.

_____ Puritans

_____ Massachusetts Bay Colony

_____ symbolism

_____ Nathaniel Hawthorne

_____ theme

_____ blank verse

_____ setting

_____ characterization

_____ morality

Write a sentence that includes one term you know from the list. Make certain that your sentence shows that you know the meaning of the term.

When a signal is given to move from your seat, find someone in the class who can tell you what a term you are uncertain of means. Write that explanation down.

Figure 4–6

Name _____ Date _____

Prereading List for Poetry

Place a "T" next to the terms you know well enough to teach to someone else.

Place an "H: next to the terms you have heard of.

Place a question mark "?" next to terms that are new to you.

_____ meter

_____ rhyme

_____ rhythm

_____ free verse

_____ imagery

_____ blank verse

_____ personification

_____ onomatopoeia

Write a sentence that includes one term you know from the list. Make certain that your sentence shows that you know the meaning of the term. If you do not know any of the terms, write one question you have about poetry.

Figure 4–7

Name _____ Date _____

Prereading List for *Romeo and Juliet*

Place a "T" next to the terms you know well enough to teach to someone else.

Place an "H" next to the terms you have heard of.

Place a question mark "?" next to terms that are new to you.

_____Shakespeare

_____monologue

_____ aside

_____ couplet

_____ Globe Theater

_____ Stratford-Upon-Avon

_____ soliloquy

_____ iambic pentameter

Write a sentence that includes one term you know from the list. Make certain that your sentence shows that you know the meaning of the term. If you do not know any of the terms, write one question you have about reading a play.

Various frameworks have been developed by psychologists and educators to consider formally the concept of how a student learns. The simplest place to begin is by learning about students' modality preferences (Saphier and Gowee 1997). Do students learn better when they see, hear, feel, or combine impressions? Chances are that middle and secondary English students either already know their personal preferences or simply need prompting to discover them. The prompt may take the form of a formal learning style inventory to discover their modality preferences. Another framework to consider is Gardner's multiple intelligence definition and theory that helps all learners to identify how they relate to knowledge and knowing (1983). Do they remember better when they sing a jingle about their assignment? Do they like to work with others? Do they have to see to believe?

It does not matter whether teachers who plan to differentiate instruction are formally cognizant of any or all of the formal frameworks. Rather, to begin to differentiate, it is most important that teachers acknowledge that individuals do learn differently and that it is their role and obligation to learn about these differences and also to help the students discover their own unique learning styles through any of the suggested strategies in Figure 4.8.

What Does Classroom Management Look Like in a Differentiated Classroom?

The maxim that good teachers lead from behind is especially true in a classroom in which lessons are differentiated. Students may be busy writing, reading, and talking, but to the casual visitor, it may appear that the teacher is not really teaching. Direct instruction, only one of many ways to deliver instruction in a differentiated classroom, may not always be apparent.

Because classes in which differentiation is practiced are student centered, the teacher may be seen moving from group to group or

Figure 4–8

Suggested Strategies for Getting to Know Students

1. Getting to Know Me

2. Getting-to-Know-You Vocabulary Sheet

3. Interest Surveys

4. Visuals. Collages, Show and Tell

5. Journal Writing

6. Interviews

7. Timed and Untimed Writing Samples

8. Standardized Test Scores

9. Self-reported Reading Survey

10. K-W-L

11. Prereading List

12. Learning Style Inventories

providing direct instruction for a small group of students or for an individual. At times the teacher may be addressing the class as a whole, or students may be presenting their work to the entire class. Having a class such as this operate smoothly does not happen by chance. Leading from behind means that the teacher must plan carefully. After the lesson or unit is planned, the managing of the day-to-day process of learning is as important as the delivery of instruction. Concern with classroom management can stop teachers from trying new approaches to teaching and learning.

Basic classroom management for differentiated classrooms is similar to management in traditional classrooms. Students need to

Figure 4–9

Classroom Agreements

As members of this class, we agree to:

Check the board daily for instructions

Maintain records in our work folders

Complete all work on schedule

Help move desks when needed, quickly and quietly

Listen and share when working in groups

Talk quietly when working in groups

Wait our turn and not interrupt the teacher or other students

Do the best work we can

know the class expectations and the consequences for not adhering to these expectations. In addition, the teacher must explain clearly the procedures for working independently and for working cooperatively. All of these expectations and procedures should be posted in the room for students to refer to as needed (see Figure 4.9).

In addition to the procedural rules for an effective classroom, teachers can include expectations for the affective behavior of students as well. Karen O'Holla, a teacher at South Brunswick High School in New Jersey, asked her students to brainstorm behaviors and attitudes they would like to see in their classroom. These are posted on a bulletin board in her room (Figure 4.10).

Organizing resources for differentiated instruction ahead of time can help students use the class time more efficiently. For example, if students are moving from station to station during a class period, all

Figure 4–10

Behaviors and Attitudes

In our class students are:

Respectful

Courteous

Attentive

Positive

Helpful

Interested

Supportive

Inquisitive

Patient

Complimentary

Industrious

Creative

Reliable

the materials they need to complete the task at each station should be set up ahead of time. In schools in which teachers move from room to room, this preparation can be accomplished in other ways. The teacher can assign management tasks to students in the class. For example, at the beginning of the class, students can distribute the materials needed at each area. At the end of class, students can help in the cleanup process.

The workshop model for student-centered classes works well for differentiated instruction. In this model, the unit or lesson begins with the teacher and students exploring a topic or skill together. Students then break into groups or begin independent study. During the class, small groups of students or individual students may meet with the teacher for direct instruction or to review work they have done. At set times, the whole class comes together again to share their ideas, ask questions, or have closure. This pattern of whole-class work, to group and individual work, to whole-class work continues until it is time for the students to present their final products. Although students work independently and in small groups, there is still a time frame within which the work must be completed. For this model to work smoothly, the teacher has to plan carefully, monitor the students' work, and revise the plan as needed.

Anchor Activities

Because students work at different paces, the teacher needs to have anchor activities prepared for those who finish early. Anchor activities, tasks that have been designed for students to work on independently, are not busywork but tie into the topic and the skills being studied. In English classes, anchor activities might include silent reading, journal writing, essay drafting, revising, editing, grammar worksheets, and prereading activities. Anchor activities must be announced at the beginning of the unit so that the students will know how to move to these activities without interrupting the teacher, who may be working with another student or group. For example, one activity might be for students to take their writing folders out and revise a paper they have been drafting. Another anchor activity might be to practice a skill such as editing by reviewing grammar rules and then applying them in editing a paper. Practice editing sheets for punctuation and usage may be completed at a student's own pace.

Differentiated Instruction in the English Classroom

How do Teachers Keep Track of All of These Students Doing Different Things?

Record keeping is a challenge for the teacher in a differentiated classroom, but it does not have to be overwhelming. Successful record keeping actually begins with the planning stage. When teachers use a planning guide, such as one of those discussed in Chapter 6 (see Figure 6.1), they have already identified the areas of the curriculum that can be differentiated. After preassessing the students and ascertaining their learning needs, the teacher can complete a differentiated learning plan for students when needed (Figure 4.11). After students have reviewed the plan, it is their responsibility to keep a record of the work they complete. The plan should contain the goals, a timeline, a student record-keeping system, a schedule for meeting with the teacher, and a defined conclusion or final product. At times, the differentiated plan may be for pairs or small groups of students as well as individuals.

One form of student record keeping that is familiar to many English teachers is a work folder or portfolio of student work. Students are responsible for keeping their work folders complete. In the folders are student work samples, peer or teacher feedback on work, a notation of any conferences held, and a calendar or timeline. Strickland and Strickland (2002) offer a model of record keeping that can be adapted for many language arts activities (Figure 4.12). Teachers do not have to complete a record for each student each day; they can select specific students to watch on any given day, but it is essential that all students be monitored consistently and evenly.

Figure 4–11

Differentiated Learning Plan

Student's Name _____ Date _____

Unit of Study _____

I agree to complete the following assignment:

The product(s) I will submit are:

My time frame for completing this work is:

My work will be assessed based on:

The consequences if I do not fulfill my contract are:

Signature of Student _____ Date _____

Signature of Teacher _____ Date _____

Figure 4–12 Model of Record Keeping

Student Name (Title of Work)	Conf date	Focus Thesis	Open- ing	Organi- zation	Develop- ment	Transi- tions	Sentence structure	Conclu- sion	Usage Issues	Comments
Ashley (mod. art)	3/21	+	+	✓	✓	-	-	-	✓	strong intro. Needs an ending. work on trans.
Laura (Soap opera)	3/21	✓	-	-	-	NA	NA	NA	NA	first draft. discussed notice. suggest outlines
Benjamin (acting)	3/23	+	+	+	✓	+	✓	✓	-	almost ready. needs to clean up some loc's; edit
Jason (security)	3/23	+	-	+	+	+	+	✓	✓	still needs a catchy opening to draw reader
Kim untitled	3/23	-	-	-	NA	NA	NA	NA	NA	struggling to find a topic or focus
Alicia (Reporting)	3/23	+	+	✓	✓	✓	+	-	NA	good start but loose ✓statement; suggest freewriting
Kelly (health care)	3/25	+	+	+	+	+	-	+	+	Could work on variety of sentences; begin new

Symbol Explanation:

+ well developed

✓ satisfactory

− needs attention

NA not applicable

Reprinted from *Engaged in Learning: Teaching English, 6–12* by Kathleen Strickland and James Strickland. Copyright © 2002 by Kathleen and James Srickland. Published by Heinemann, a division of Reed Elsevier, Inc., Portsmouth, NH.

What Do Specific Examples of Differentiated Instruction Look Like in the English Classroom?

Differentiated instruction is not a formula for teaching; it is a philosophy about learning. As such, there can be no blueprint to follow in order to create the perfect differentiated classroom. However, teachers take their philosophy of education and their beliefs about teaching and learning and put them into practice in the differentiated instruction classroom. In doing so, they develop strategies for teaching and learning. This chapter offers examples of strategies English teachers commonly use when differentiating lessons. The strategies, offered here in alphabetical order, are not meant to exhaust the list of activities and assignments that can support differentiated instruction; they are simply ones that middle and secondary English teachers have used successfully (see Figure 5.1). It is important to remember that no matter which strategy is employed, all of the students in a class should be working toward the same goal.

Figure 5–1

Strategies That Support Differentiated Instruction

- Alternative Assignments: student choice, learning styles
- Anchor Activities
- Curriculum Compacting
- Flexible Grouping
- Homework Assignments
- Independent Study and Learning Contracts
- Jigsaw Activities
- Learning Stations
- Literature Circles
- Multiple Texts
- Performance Assessments
- Research Projects
- Socratic Seminar
- Tic-Tac-Toe Assignments
- Tiered Assignments
- WebQuests
- Writing Workshop

Alternative Assignments: Student Choice

Student choice is a key component when incorporating differentiated instruction into a unit or lesson. Many English teachers already use some form of student choice in their assignments. For example, teachers may require outside reading; that is, they ask students to read a book of their choice independently outside of class during a marking period or semester. Students then report on the book orally or in writing. In addition, teachers may build a choice of topics into writing assignments; for example, when students are writing a persuasive paper they can select an issue about which they have strong opinions.

Alternative Assignments: Learning Styles

Teachers can develop assignments based on student differences in learning styles. Assignments can include various ways for students to represent their understanding of a text they have read. Students might represent the message or main idea of a poem in the form of a drawing, a dramatic presentation, or a written analysis. Alternative assignments can be assigned by the teacher or selected by the student. Teachers may assign lessons based on student readiness, interests, or learning styles, or they may give the students the option of selecting from a list of assignments. Alternative assignments also can be student-designed. A teacher can challenge learners to create and design assignments based on a particular theme, reading, or concept.

Anchor Activities

Anchor activities are activities that students can work on when they finish an assignment before their classmates or when they have free time, for example, when they are waiting for a conference with the teacher or a peer. Anchor activities are not busywork; they are meaningful activities that give the students practice in applying the skills and concepts they have learned. Anchor activities should be assignments that students can work on independently and that can be taken up and put down without interruption. For example, in the English class, anchor activities can include reading, using a computer for writing or researching, illustrating a work read, using the Internet, revising and editing written work, writing in a journal, or creating word games.

Curriculum Compacting

By compacting the curriculum, students who already have mastered some concepts and skills can be accelerated based on readiness. There are times when students do not need to learn everything planned for a unit because they already know some, if not all, of the material being studied. When teachers begin a unit, they first ascertain what prior knowledge their students possess. If any student already knows much of the material, the teacher can compact or compress the curriculum. First the teacher gives a test or other form of preassessment to identify any students who already know the material. Some students may be able to complete the planned curriculum in a shortened or compacted amount of time. For these students, the teacher develops individual plans that take them beyond the basics of the unit to an investigation or application of the main concepts or skills (in the curriculum being studied in the class). In any given unit, only part of the information and skills may be new for some students. The curriculum can be compacted in the areas they know, but they can participate with the rest of the class in other areas of the unit.

Compacting in the English language arts classroom works best for skills lessons. When studying skills such as grammar, mechanics, spelling, or usage, students may "compact out" of skills minilessons and concentrate on applying these skills. For example, if during a writing unit that includes studying the punctuation of compound-complex sentences several students demonstrate on a pretest that they can correctly punctuate such sentences, the

Differentiated Instruction in the English Classroom

teacher can work with these students to develop an alternative two-week plan. While the class is receiving direct instruction and practice in the correct use of commas and semicolons in compound-complex sentences, the students who "compacted out" can be working on one of their long-range writing projects with an emphasis on revising to include more sentence variety. These students are working on an assignment that the whole class has to complete, but they are focusing on a higher level of sentence construction in context. This way they are doing not more work, but a level of work that fits their readiness. Compacting can also be used for skills associated with reading and literature. For example, if a teacher has planned to spend the first part of a poetry unit on introducing and explaining literary devices such as personification, metaphor, simile, or onomatopoeia, and a student has shown on a pretest that he or she already can define and explain these terms, that student should work with the teacher to develop a compacting contract for advanced study (see Figure 5.2). This study could include the reading of more challenging poems than those being used to teach the literary devices in class. Again, this student is doing not more work, but a different level of work.

Flexible Grouping

Flexible grouping is fundamental to differentiated instruction classrooms. In flexible grouping, students move into and out of groups either by choice or by teacher assignment. Groups may consist of up to six students. Students work with many different classmates during a unit of study because groups do not stay the same for a long period of time. For example, when studying a unit on Lorraine Hansberry's *A Raisin in the Sun*, a student may work with a partner of a different level of readiness when selecting and explaining quotations in the play. The same student may be part of

Figure 5–2

Curriculum Compacting Agreement

Student's Name: Robin Magnusen   **Teacher's Name:** Mr. Zabrinski

Unit: Poetry   **Grade/Level:** 11

Knowledge/Skills Mastered

Understanding of poetic devices:
    metaphor, extended metaphor, simile, personificaton, alliteration, onomatopoeia, tone

Evidence of Mastery

    Pretest to define and give examples of each poetic device

Learning Plan

1. Student selects 10 poems with teacher approval.
2. Student keeps a poetry response journal, making entries for each poem: reactions to, interpretations of, and questions about poems.
3. Poetry journal entries identify poetic devices used in each poem.
4. Student selects three poems for written analysis.
5. Student writes analyses of how literary devices used in these poems help to develop their meaning and tone.

Resources Needed

    Anthologies of poetry from classroom library

Completion Date

    a week before the end of the third marking period

Product(s) to be submitted

    Poetry response journal

    Three written literary analyses of poems selected, following format reviewed in class

Student's Signature and Date _____

Teacher's Signature and Date _____

a small group of students with similar learning styles who design stage sets for a production of the drama. Also during the same unit, this student may work with another group of students with the same demonstrated level of readiness to write a critique of a performance. This writing group may meet with the teacher for mini-lessons and feedback sessions while they are completing the assignment.

Homework Assignments

Many teachers begin differentiating assignments by creating more than one homework assignment or different levels of the same assignment. This is especially useful if the class contains students who are at different levels of readiness. For example, students may respond to different questions after reading a text, or they may read different poems from the unit. After reading the short story "The Secret Life of Walter Mitty," some students may be ready to write and answer their own open-ended questions, while others need more practice responding to open-ended questions that are already prepared.

Independent Study and Learning Contracts

Independent study gives students the opportunity to pursue something in-depth that they want to know more about. Independent study can be offered to students who wish to investigate a subject in which they have a sincere interest or to those who have already mastered the unit's content and are ready to pursue advanced information and concepts.

Independent study begins when the teacher and student identify an area and agree on a plan, timeline, and final product. Independent study projects can be completed during class time if the student has "compacted" out of the unit or part of the unit, or they can be completed outside the class during the student's own time. Most independent projects include a learning contract, a formal agreement between the teacher and the student. Learning contracts contain goals, timelines, and a plan for the final product (Figure 5.3) and are signed by both the student and the teacher. The assessment of the final product must be specified at the beginning of the study. A shared rubric to define expectations can be mutually developed by student and teacher. The emphasis in an independent study should be on *independence*. It should not require a large amount of additional work for the teacher. Independent projects in the English class may vary greatly, from completing a creative writing portfolio to producing a short film.

Jigsaw Activities

Jigsaw is a popular cooperative learning strategy that divides the material to be studied into sections and makes individuals or groups responsible for learning and then teaching their section to the other students. In the most common form of jigsaw, students belong to both a home group and an expert group. Students do not become members of an expert group because they have prior knowledge in that area, but because in the course of studying the topic with other students, they will become experts. Each member of the home group leaves that group to spend time with the expert group. In their expert groups, students study new information and then return to share it with their home groups. This strategy works well in a differentiated classroom because the teacher can assign material to each expert group, based on student interests or readiness. For example, if students are studying *Hamlet*, each expert group can follow one character throughout the play. Students who are more capable might study Hamlet himself, while less-ready

Differentiated Instruction in the English Classroom

Figure 5–3

Independent Learning Contract

Student's Name: Justine Wood   **Teacher's Name:** Barbara King-Shaver

Topic/Text: *Hamlet* by William Shakespeare

Reason for Contract: prior knowledge, readiness

Time frame: Beginning Date: 1/30/01   Completion Date: 2/20/01

Independent Assignment:

During independent study time, I will go to the media center to research feminist literary criticism on Shakespeare's *Hamlet*, using both written and on-line sources. I will then spend five class periods reading, taking notes, and writing a review of criticism. When the class has finished reading the play, I will share my findings with them in an oral report. I will also submit a written paper to my teacher.

Products: oral report, written paper

Assessment:

Oral report will be assessed using the class speaking rubric.
Paper will be assessed by teacher using written comments.

Student's Signature and Date _____

Teacher's Signature and Date _____

students might be given his mother as their character. When members of the expert groups return to their home groups, each student reports on his/her character's motivation and development. After all students have reported, the group has a better understanding of all major characters in *Hamlet*.

The jigsaw strategy can be used for skill lessons. Based on readiness, students in the home groups can be assigned to an expert group on punctuation, with each expert group focusing on a different form of punctuation. More advanced students do commas; less advanced do question marks. These "experts" then return to their home groups and explain how to use their punctuation symbol correctly. Jigsaw can also be used successfully for large research topics and outside readings, and it can be used between English classes. For example, classes can read difficult plays or acts of the same play and serve as "experts" to other classes.

Learning Stations

Learning stations are designed to help students learn and practice concepts or skills. When using learning stations, students move from one area of the room to another to complete different tasks at each station. Learning stations are different from the permanently established activity centers that are used in many elementary classrooms. Learning stations are areas designed for working on a series of assignments for a specified period of time. Depending on student readiness, interest, or learning styles, some stations may be required for all students, and others may be optional. In addition, freedom of choice of stations may be built into some assignments. For example, when studying persuasive writing, the teacher may create five stations in the classroom and require every student to complete each station. One station asks that students analyze three magazine advertisements, identifying the strategies used in the advertisement to persuade the reader. At a second station, students complete a worksheet on the main types of persuasive devices. A third station requires students to read a brief essay and highlight the persuasive devices used. At a fourth station, students create their own persuasive advertisement for a

Differentiated Instruction in the English Classroom

magazine. A fifth station asks students to brainstorm topics for a persuasive essay.

Literature Circles

Literature circles support differentiation because of their emphasis on student choice and their use of multiple texts to support differentiation based on readiness and interest. Although there are a variety of models for using literature circles, Daniels (1994) developed a model that is widely used in English classes. Literature circles combine cooperative learning and independent reading. Students select the work they wish to read and discuss. They may select the work from a teacher-prepared list or from outside texts. Literature circle groups meet for a specified period of time to discuss a book, poem, short story, or article read in common. In his original model, Daniels assigns specific roles to each member of the group, at least in the beginning until students are comfortable with the discussion groups. These roles often include discussion director, literary luminary, connector, illustrator, word master, and character captain (Daniels 1994, 62). The roles rotate each time the group meets. By using literature circles in the class, an English teacher can offer a range of titles for the students to read and offer learners a variety of interpretive experiences and roles.

Multiple Texts

Students may be assigned to read different texts connected by theme or genre or to select a text from a list of possible titles. After they have read the texts, the students produce an artifact such as a book report or speech. In another variation, several students may read the same text so that groups of students who have read a text in common can then meet and participate in discussions, much like those conducted in literature circles. For example, students for whom *Roots* may be too challenging may be given the option to read *The Glory Field* or *The Watsons Go to Birmingham*. Teachers frequently have collections of multiple texts in their classrooms from which students may choose their readings.

Performance Assessments

Performance assessments provide students with the opportunity to demonstrate their learning through a variety of products in different modes. For this reason, performance assessments can support differentiation based on both readiness and learning styles. Insofar as possible, performance assessments try to duplicate activities in which people engage in the world outside of school. Rubrics or scoring guides accompany performance assessments so students can have a clear understanding of how their products will be assessed. Performance assessments may be small activities within or at the end of a classroom unit, or they can be major course requirements across the school. An example of the former would be having students create an anthology of poems around a central theme and include open-ended questions about the poems. An example of the latter would be requiring all seniors to research a topic and to give written and oral presentations of their findings as a graduation requirement.

Research Projects

Many English teachers assign research projects or papers at some point during the school year. Often student choice is built into the selection of topic. This practice can support differentiated instruction based on student interest. With guidance from the teacher, the topic can also connect to student readiness. For example, the

Differentiated Instruction in the English Classroom

teacher can prepare a range of topics and arrange them by level of difficulty. Each student is directed to select from an assigned level of topics, depending on readiness. When differentiating the research assignment according to student interests, the model for *I-Search* papers developed by Macrorie (1988) works well in a differentiated classroom. Using this model, each student conducts an inquiry, based on a topic of personal interest, posing the research questions and conducting the research, before writing a paper. The topics of these papers are wide-ranging and not the typical academic ones. For example, one student might be investigating the art of crocheting while another researches the influences of bluegrass on rock music.

Socratic Seminar

Socratic Seminar is a discussion strategy that emphasizes thoughtful dialogue among the students without teacher intervention. It is based on the Socratic questioning model adapted for classrooms by Adler of the *Paideia Proposal* (1982). Classroom teachers have developed variations on Socratic Seminar. In one model, all students sit in a circle and participate in an open-ended discussion. The teacher serves as the moderator and may also pose the questions to be discussed. Another variation on this model is to have the students pose the questions. Some teachers ask students to prepare open-ended questions ahead of time. In a second configuration, students sit in two concentric circles, with the inner circle discussing a topic or text and the outer circle observing (Ball and Brewer 2000). Halfway through the discussion, the two circles trade places. A variation on this model is to have the students in the outer circle give feedback to those in the inner circle.

Although Socratic Seminars may be issue-centered, they are best when focused on a particular text that the students have read in common. Some English teachers include near the end of every unit a Socratic Seminar that features a major work of literature, such as a novel or a play. They also use it within a unit after a close reading of a shorter text such as a poem or an essay. Socratic Seminar strategies support differentiated instruction because teachers can assign or require learners to develop questions from different levels of Bloom's taxonomy (1956). In addition, Socratic Seminars can be used instead of literature circles when students are working in small groups to discuss different texts.

Tic-Tac-Toe Assignments

Classroom teachers have found using the Tic-Tac-Toe board to be a positive way to present a variety of assignments (Figure 5.4). The assignments on the board may be arranged by rows representing degree of difficulty or by rows representing learning preferences. Students must complete a Tic-Tac-Toe board by selecting and completing three assignments in a row by the end of the unit. A row of choices for a unit on *To Kill A Mockingbird*, for example, might include writing a journal that Scout would have kept, writing a letter of apology to Boo, or writing a persuasive letter convincing ninth graders to read this important novel. Another row might include drawing a crucial scene from the novel and explaining why it was chosen, creating costumes for a film version of the novel and explaining how they reflect the characters, or selecting music to accompany scenes of the novel and explaining why the pieces were chosen.

A variation of Tic-Tac-Toe is to use the board for extension activities for students who have demonstrated the ability to go beyond the core class assignments. Winebrenner (2002), the authority on the education of gifted and talented, who developed the original Tic-Tac-Toe Menu for organizing extension activities,

Figure 5–4

Tic-Tac-Toe Activity

Student Directions: Select and complete three activities, vertically or diagonally, to make Tic-Tac-Toe.

Hamlet

Design the costumes for a stage production of *Hamlet* that is set in a period other than the one which it was written. Be prepared to explain your designs.	Design the sets for a stage production of *Hamlet* that takes place in a period other than the one in which it was written. Be prepared to explain your set designs.	Cast the actors for a new American film of *Hamlet*. For each character selected, write an explanation for your choice.
Keep a log of quotations (five for each act). Explain the meaning of each and its significance in developing plot, character, and theme.	Keep a log of motifs as they appear in each act. Explain how each works to develop plot, character, and theme.	Keep a log that traces a Freudian reading of the play. Identify and explain speeches and actions that support such an interpretation.
Write an essay proving or disproving the claim that Hamlet is mad.	Write an essay on the view of women presented in *Hamlet*.	Write an essay discussing how Laertes serves as a foil to Hamlet.

Prepared by Barbara King-Shaver, Ed. D.

now calls it the Extension Menu. Students do not necessarily need to complete more than one activity when the menu is used as an "extension." Tomlinson (2001) has developed a variation of Tic-Tac-Toe for novel study called Think-Tac-Toe that asks students to complete three of the assignments on the board, not necessarily in a line.

Tiered Assignments

When teachers want "to ensure that students with different learning needs work with the same essential ideas and use the same key skills," tiered assignments are used (Tomlinson 1999, 83). By using tiered assignments, students can take different paths to reach common goals. Teachers create tiered assignments based on student readiness and prior knowledge. The levels of complexity of the tasks may vary, but the overarching understandings and core skills are the same. Teachers might envision a ladder with assignments requiring a higher level of complexity at the top; they can then differentiate assignments moving down the ladder (Tomlinson 1999). When studying a Shakespearean play, for example, the less capable readers may be asked to keep a double-entry journal with quotations on the left-hand side of the page and their observations and/or questions about the quotations in the right-hand column. For the same section of the play, the more advanced readers may be asked to explicate the quotation with an emphasis on the literary devices used to create meaning. In this example, all students are practicing the skill of close reading of a text as they build understanding of the plot and characters. Both of these assignments can be teacher-directed, requiring that certain quotations be located, or they might be more open-ended, allowing the students to select the quotations.

WebQuests

WebQuests are inquiry-based activities designed by teachers to help students effectively negotiate the Internet for a teacher-assigned or student-selected topic. When creating WebQuests, the teacher predetermines Internet links that are connected to the agreed-upon topic. Because teachers predetermine the Internet links, WebQuests are a good introduction to research using the World Wide Web. They also help students avoid accessing inappropriate material. WebQuests support differentiated instruction because they can be based on student readiness and interest and can be conducted as a group or individual inquiry. Students begin a WebQuest with a central question to be answered. In answering this question, they research real resources available on the World Wide Web. For example, students might be reading *One Flew Over the Cuckoo's Nest* as part of a thematic unit on mental health and begin their WebQuests with the questions: Has the treatment of patients in public mental health facilities changed since this book was written? If so, how? What brought about these changes? For this WebQuest, the teacher might create Web links to sites that explain the history and use of electric shock therapy for mental illness, the legal requirements for committing someone to a mental hospital, or the training of psychiatric care nurses. A good site at which to begin research for mental health issues related to *One Flew Over the Cuckoo's Nest* is www.nimh.gov/publict/index.cfm. WebQuests are available online or can be created by individual teachers. An online source for English teachers is www.webenglishteacher.com.

Writing Workshop

In a writing workshop, students work at their own pace on the various stages of the writing process: prewriting, drafting, revising, and editing. They may be working individually, in pairs, in small groups, or in conferences with the teacher. In one class period, a group of students may be giving feedback to each other on the papers they have drafted while another group of students is brainstorming ideas for their next papers. When these students are working in groups, others may be drafting or editing their papers individually, and the teacher may be holding a conference with a student who has just completed a draft of a paper. Additionally, the teacher may provide minilessons on writing and editing during the writing workshop.

All of the strategies discussed above can be used within a unit of study; however, it is best for the sanity of the students and the teacher to limit the number of options that will be presented at any one time. As with all forms of differentiation, alternative assignments, different ways to reach an identified goal, are offered only after the need and purpose for each one has been clearly established.

How Do Teachers Put It All Together? A Case Study with Examples

T his chapter provides a model for implementing differentiated instruction in a secondary English Department by looking at one school, South Brunswick High School, a large suburban high school located in central New Jersey. Each class described in these examples meets every other day in a block period for 84 minutes. The English teachers whose lessons are presented in this chapter attended one or more professional development opportunities on the topic of differentiated instruction. The planning guide the teachers used, based on the essential questions model of Wiggins and McTighe (1998) and the content, process, product model of Tomlinson (1999), represents the last step in planning differentiated lessons (see Figure 6.1). As noted earlier, teachers must first decide why they are going to differentiate and then which students would benefit from differentiated work. After this has been done, lesson planning can begin. Each of the examples presented in this chapter contains a planning guide, a description of the English class, and a class assignment.

Figure 6–1

The Basic Planning Guide

Course Title and Level:

Unit:

Essential Questions:

Unit-Specific Questions:

Knowledge/Skills:

Modes of Differentiation Used:

Differentiate: (content, process, product)

Based on: (readiness, interests, learning styles)

Strategies:

Assignment(s):

Differentiating Topics and Using Stations in Ninth-Grade Basic English

Planning Guide

Course/Level: Basic English I

Unit: *Romeo and Juliet* by William Shakespeare

Essential Questions:
How are the events and culture of an author's time reflected in the work of literature he/she produces?
How do researchers identify and use a variety of tools for investigating and presenting information?

Unit-Specific Question:
How are Shakespeare's life and the times in which he lived reflected in the plays he wrote?

Knowledge/Skills:
Students will know:

- The history of the Elizabethan time period
- The life of William Shakespeare
- The life and reign of Queen Elizabeth the First

Students will be able to:

- Investigate a single topic in-depth
- Conduct research using both print and Internet sources
- Arrange the research into a well-organized presentation
- Cite sources in M.L.A. format
- Learn from each other's presentations

Modes of Differentiation Used:

Differentiate:

content: Students are assigned different research topics, matching the readiness of the students to the difficulty of the topics.

process: Students are given flexible time in which to complete the project. Those who finish early have anchor activities to complete. In addition, students create and review material in learning stations in the room.

Based on: readiness

Strategies: pairs, learning stations, anchor activity

Basic English I: Differentiating Topics and Using Stations

Molly Oehrlein, a ninth- and tenth-grade English teacher, began her unit on *Romeo and Juliet* by telling the students that, to help them understand and appreciate a famous play by William Shakespeare, some basic background information would be helpful. She told them they would be responsible for teaching the class important information about a topic related to Shakespeare and to *Romeo and Juliet*. "To do this, you and a partner will create a learning center so that other students can read and learn about your topic. You will have two class blocks in which to use the library and the Internet for researching your topic. You will then have a class block in which to prepare your learning station material before it is presented to the whole class."

The topics the students researched were Shakespeare's life, Shakespeare's poems and plays, the Globe Theater, Elizabethan costumes, Queen Elizabeth I, Elizabethan England, The Black Plague, and Elizabethan weapons and armor. As they worked, the students were instructed to keep track of their sources and to find

Differentiated Instruction in the English Classroom

at least two visuals that could be copied to accompany their presentations.

On day 1 in the library, Jamie and Rodrigo found books that had information, including pictures, on their topic, Elizabethan armor and weapons. Jamie photocopied the pictures while Rodrigo went on-line to find more examples and download pictures from that site. Molly reminded the boys that they now had plenty of visuals and needed to start taking notes on the information that went with these pictures. Molly saw the same pattern of research with several pairs; therefore, at the beginning of day 2, she did a minilesson in the library about how to take notes from written information found on-line and in books. Jamie and Rodrigo spent the rest of the class on the second day reading and taking notes. Near the end of the block, they worked together and began to organize their information into categories.

For the third class, all students met in the classroom to prepare their learning stations. Molly reminded the students that they would be acting as the teachers; they were responsible for creating learning stations that contained written and visual information for their classmates. The learning stations had to be ready for the next class. During this class time, Jamie and Rodrigo began by cutting out pictures of weapons and armor they had photocopied. They then had to make decisions about how many to include. Jamie went to one of the computers in the room to create labels while Rodrigo glued the pictures to a poster board. After they had their visuals in place, they checked their notes and decided what they wanted to include in their written information. Jamie and Rodrigo decided that the pictures and captions told a lot and they would just write two paragraphs of facts each. This typed information was cut out and glued to the poster board with the pictures. The preparing of the learning stations took the whole block of class time, but by the end, Jamie and Rodrigo's poster board was ready.

At the beginning of class on the fourth day, the students set up their presentations in learning centers around the room. Molly instructed them, "Each of you will move from station to station and complete an information sheet as you go. At each station, you are to read all of the facts presented about the topic. Decide which facts are most important, and write down four of these for each section. Look over the visuals carefully, and add two more facts or inferences based on the visuals."

The students were then given a fact sheet to complete as they went from station to station (see Figure 6.2). This day the students moved individually from station to station, no longer working in pairs. When they completed their fact sheets, they returned to their desks.

When she had used stations previously, Molly rang a bell after six to eight minutes, indicating that it was time for each group to move to the next station. This time she let the students move at their own pace because she found that some students needed more time at particular stations than other students. To avoid wasted time if some students finished early, Molly used an anchor activity: students who finished early were instructed to read silently their individual outside reading selections for the marking period.

Molly noted that pairing students based on readiness, identifying the difficulty of the assignments, and allowing the students to move from station to station at their own pace created a more successful assignment. She found that her students were more confident and more engaged in the lesson than they had been previously. She also noted that they were genuinely proud of their work. In addition she found that by revising this lesson based on differentiated instruction practices, she became more reflective and flexible in her planning.

Figure 6–2

Name _____ Date _____

Learning Stations: Shakespeare

Shakespeare's Life	Shakespeare's Poems and Plays	The Globe Theater	Elizabethan Costumes
Queen Elizabeth I	Elizabethan England	The Black Plague	Elizabethan Weapons and Armor

Prepared by Molly Oehrlein

Differentiating Lessons Using Work Folders in a Skills-Based English Class

Planning Guide

Course: Skills Lab

Unit: Improving Reading of Persuasive Texts

Essential Questions:
What skills and strategies help students improve as readers?
How can students learn to monitor their own reading and writing process?
What persuasive strategies do writers include in their texts to express their opinions?

Knowledge/Skills:
Students will know:

- Their own strengths and needs as readers
- The purpose and form of persuasive texts
- Persuasive devices used by authors

Students will be able to:

- Monitor their own reading process
- Identify and understand persuasive strategies when they appear in a text

Modes of Differentiation Used:

Differentiate:

content: different genre, levels of reading material, student choice in reading selections

Differentiated Instruction in the English Classroom

process: curriculum compacting for a student who is more advanced in reading performance but still needs practice applying reading skills and strategies to a variety of genre, small group work, independent work

products: reader response logs, graphic organizers

Based on: readiness and interests

Strategies: curriculum compacting, tiering, student choice

Skills Lab: Differentiating Lessons Using Work Folders

Lisa, a 16-year-old eleventh grader, enters the skills lab classroom and retrieves her folder from the filing cabinet. She reviews her work from the previous day and checks her assignment sheet to see what has to be completed next (Figure 6.3). Her teacher is gathering three students together to meet with her at a table for direct instruction in identifying information to support the main idea in a persuasive essay.

Lisa's folder contains more advanced work on reading and responding to persuasive essays because, based on her preassessment for this unit, she has compacted out of the basic lesson. Lisa takes a persuasive essay from her folder and, following the directions her teacher has placed in the folder, reads the essay through twice. The first time she reads for overall meaning; the second time she reads to identify persuasive techniques used in the essay. When Lisa finds a persuasive device used, she enters it into her reading log, along with an explanation of how it works to persuade the reader. When her teacher is finished working with the small group, the students go back to their desks to read, and she meets with Lisa to review the entries she has made in her log. The teacher asks Lisa to explain why she identified the words as persuasive.

Figure 6–3

Name _____ Date _____ Session # _____

Daily Agreement

Activity	Date Started	Date Completed	Skills/ Strategies I Learned	Skills/ Strategies I Still Need to Work On	How I Can Use These Skills in Other Learning Situations
Reading Comprehension					
Written Composition					
Vocabulary					

Developed by Rhonda Slawinski

Differentiated Instruction in the English Classroom

After the teacher is assured that Lisa understands these persuasive devices, she introduces a graphic organizer for Lisa to complete that outlines the organization of the essay. Lisa then returns to her seat to begin filling in the graphic organizer.

Puneet is one of the students who met with the teacher in the small group. Because he recently left an English as a Second Language (ESL) class, Puneet's reading assignment is more basic than those the other students are reading. When he returns to his seat after meeting in the group, Puneet reads a letter to the editor from a local paper while most of his classmates are reading a longer persuasive article from *Time* magazine. As he reads, Puneet keeps a split-entry reading log. On the left-hand side of the log, he enters any words or phrases that are unclear to him. On the right-hand side, he writes the meaning of the words from a dictionary and/or a question he has about the meaning and use of the words and phrases in this letter. When he meets with the teacher, they review his log together, and she helps him understand some of the language that is unclear. Puneet and the teacher review what his next assignment will be.

The teacher then instructs the whole class to put away their work folders and take out their independent reading books. For the last 15 minutes of class, everyone participates in Sustained Silent Reading (SSR). The students select books for SSR from the class library, or they bring them from home to read.

Using individual folders allows the teacher to implement both learning contracts and curriculum compacting because students work at their own pace on different levels of reading. The teacher has tiered the assignment, identifying less challenging texts for students such as Puneet, and more challenging texts for students such as Lisa. The folders help students maintain a record of their own progress in the class. They can readily see in which areas they have been successful, and in which areas they need more practice or instruction. In addition, the folders are a good way to organize lessons based on curriculum compacting. This independent work can be done without disturbing the rest of the class.

Many English departments offer lab courses for students who need instruction in and a review of basic reading and writing skills and strategies. At South Brunswick High School, students are placed in a skills lab based on a preassessment of their reading and writing abilities. This course is taken in addition to a regular English class. The goals of the skills labs in South Brunswick High School are to help students become better readers and writers so that they can be successful in all of their courses and to help them be better prepared for the state language arts proficiency assessment.

Because of the nature of the course, preassessment is a key component. Typical preassessments include a practice state test, including a timed writing sample; a review of previous standardized test scores; a review of the student's writing portfolio; and a personal reflection on how the student sees himself or herself as a reader and writer. After this information is obtained, the content of the course is planned to address student needs. In one class, students may be working on different skills and at different levels of difficulty. Differentiated instruction is a necessity in such a classroom.

Differentiating Content Using Stations in a Tenth-Grade English Class

Planning Guide

Course Title and Level: English II Honors

Unit: *The Crucible* by Arthur Miller

Essential Questions:
What causes mass hysteria?
When is it worth risking one's life for one's principles?
How does an historical event become transformed into a work of literature?
How does an author use literary devices to convey meaning?

Unit-Specific Questions:
How relevant is *The Crucible* to today's world?
How do Miller's diction and imagery convey his meaning?

Knowledge/Skills:
Student will know:

- The historical background of the Puritan times
- The historical background of the McCarthy era
- Miller's writing style
- How authors create memorable characters

Students will be able to:

- Make connections between modern times and historical events
- Characterize the main characters in the play
- Explain the choices John Proctor makes
- Explain how Miller's language supports his message
- Use new vocabulary words.

Modes of Differentiation Used:

Differentiate:

process: By using learning stations, students can work at their own pace. In addition, some choice is included in the learning station assignments. An anchor activity is provided for students who may finish before the end of the class.

product: written paragraphs, drawings, graphic organizers, worksheets

Based on: interests and learning styles

Strategies: learning stations, anchor activity

English II: Differentiating Content Using Stations

As students enter her sophomore honors English class, the teacher, Karen O'Holla, distributes instruction sheets to each student. The instruction sheets explain the learning station activity for the day's lesson (Figure 6.4). She also gives students a folder into which they can place their work. Karen tells the students that they must complete the first three (of six) stations but have their choice of one of the last three stations. These stations do not have to be completed in any particular order, allowing for students to spread out among them. If students finish before class time is up, they are instructed to return to their seats and read an article on McCarthyism that is found in their folders.

Keisha takes one of the learning station instruction sheets and moves immediately to station four, where the teacher has various sizes of paper and markers, colored pencils, and pens. Keisha has always liked to draw, so she decides to use colored markers to create a drawing of the courtroom scene. She then places her drawing

Differentiated Instruction in the English Classroom

Figure 6–4

Instruction Sheet for *The Crucible* Learning Stations

Station One:

At this station you will read an article containing historical information about the event depicted in *The Crucible*. Take a worksheet from the station and complete it by identifying three events or facts from the play that are very close to historical events. Next, identify two events or facts that have been changed to a large extent.

Station Two:

Assume the role of John Proctor and write a letter to your young children to read when they are older. The letter should explain why you made the decision you did at the end of the play.

Station Three:

Use six of the vocabulary cards of words taken from the play to write a paragraph or poem.

Station Four:

Create a visual representation for a scene in the play, or design a costume for one of the main characters.

Station Five:

Write four open-ended, higher-level thoughtful questions on the play.

Station Six:

Complete a character graphic organizer on one of the main characters in the play. You can select the character and you may use the computer.

into her folder, checks that station off on her instruction sheet, and moves to station 1. Here Keisha quietly reads a copy of the article on the historical facts of *The Crucible*. She then completes the worksheet that accompanies this article.

While Keisha and several other students are reading the article, her teacher is moving around the room, reminding students to talk quietly as they move from station to station so that they will not disturb their classmates. Keisha checks off station 1 and then moves on to station 2, but because too many students are already there, she goes to station 3. Here she shares vocabulary cards with other students at the station and, using six vocabulary words, writes a paragraph about how unfair the trial in the play was. There is some talking and sharing of ideas with other students at this station.

When she finishes at station 3, there is room at station 6, and Keisha moves on to that area. She completes a graphic organizer that asks her to identify the traits of one of the main characters in the play and to support each trait with an example. There are copies of the play on the table. It takes time to look up examples, and Keisha looks at the clock. When she does finish this station activity, Keisha asks her teacher what happens if she does not finish all four stations today. Her teacher tells Keisha to keep working until she calls time. She will then give the students further directions if they are not finished with the stations. Keisha is in the midst of completing station 2 when time is called.

With five minutes left in the class, Karen asks everyone to return to their seats so that she can collect all the work folders. Karen frequently has time limits at each station to keep students moving at the same pace. For this lesson, however, she decides to watch and see how engaged the students are and how many complete all stations by the end of class. On this day, she observes that all are busy right until the end of the class, so she extends the activity for half of the next class block. Teachers who practice differentiated instruction learn to be flexible.

Learning stations support differentiated instruction by offering direct instruction as needed, presenting student choice, and addressing a variety of learning styles. Karen O'Holla is an experienced teacher who teaches both standard and honors English courses. She is a proponent of learning stations, and she incorporates them frequently into all levels of her sophomore classes. Karen uses stations for both skills work and literature lessons; in fact, she often integrates skill activities with literature. In addition, Karen always tries to include at least one station that contains a more creative activity, such as drawing, so that students with different learning styles have an opportunity to display their learning and their talents.

Karen sees organization as key when using learning stations, and she offers advice for teachers who are planning to implement them. Teachers must work out the logistics ahead of time in order for students to benefit the most from the lesson. She suggests that teachers have all directions and materials ready and easily accessible, clarify the requirements for the activity, explain how student work will be graded, explain how to move from station to station, establish a plan to work with students who need extra help, provide anchor activities for students who finish early, and be flexible enough to alter time as needed. When a teacher is not giving instruction during a station activity, her job is to observe the students and keep track of their focus and effort. Karen supports the use of learning stations because she finds that it is a good way to approach many levels of learning and learning styles. She further notes that learning stations give students the opportunity to work on their own or with others while being responsible for their own success. Finally, she finds that students, "think it is fun and don't realize how hard they are actually working!"

Differentiating Content Using a Learning Contract in Twelfth-Grade English Class

Planning Guide

Course Title and Level: English IV Academic

Unit: *Hamlet* by William Shakespeare

Essential Questions:

How can indecision be both a positive and a negative thing?
How do authors use imagery to convey meaning?
How can a literary work be interpreted differently, depending on the school of literary criticism a reader adopts?

Unit-Specific Questions:
How does Shakespeare's imagery convey his meaning?
Who is responsible?
What is a "feminist" reading of this play?
Is Hamlet mad?

Knowledge/Skills:
Student will know:

- The plot of *Hamlet*
- How imagery supports meaning
- How a feminist literary critic interprets the play

Students will be able to:

- Compare a feminist and a traditional interpretation of the play
- Characterize the main characters in the play

Differentiated Instruction in the English Classroom

- Explain the choices Hamlet makes
- Explain how Shakespeare's language supports his message
- Debate who is responsible for the outcome of the play

Modes of Differentiation Used:

Differentiate:

process: creating an independent study contract with a student

product: oral report and written literary criticism paper

Based on: readiness and interest

Strategies: learning contract

English IV: Differentiating Content Using a Learning Contract

Justine entered twelfth grade at South Brunswick High School, having spent her junior year in England. When her teacher announced that the class would be studying *Hamlet*, Justine spoke to the teacher after class and explained that she had spent a considerable amount of time studying this play the previous year. In fact, she had written a comprehensive paper on Shakespeare's use of nature imagery and had seen two different productions of the play. After reviewing a copy of Justine's paper and discussing her interests, the teacher decided that Justine would be excused from participating in the first part of the unit, during which the class was scheduled to read the play section by section. Justine would rejoin the class for the second half of the unit, during which the students would be moving beyond literal comprehension to a discussion of the levels of meaning and the literary devices Shakespeare uses to create meaning. The teacher wanted to be fair to Justine and help her continue to learn, but she also wanted the whole class to have the benefit of Justine's insights during class discussions. Therefore, Justine and her teacher developed the independent learning contract shown in Figure 6.5.

Figure 6–5

Independent Learning Contract

Student's Name: Justine Wood   **Teacher's Name:** Barbara King-Shaver

Topic/Text: *Hamlet* by William Shakespeare

Reason for Contract: prior knowledge, readiness

Time frame: Beginning Date: 1/30/01   Completion Date: 2/20/01

Independent Assignment:

During independent study time, I will go to the media center to research feminist literary criticism on Shakespeare's *Hamlet*, using both written and on-line sources. I will then spend five class periods reading, taking notes, and writing a review of criticism. When the class has finished reading the play, I will share my findings with them in an oral report. I will also submit a written paper to my teacher.

Products: oral report, written paper

Assessment:

Oral report will be assessed using the class speaking rubric.
Paper will be assessed by teacher using written comments.

Student's Signature and Date _____

Teacher's Signature and Date _____

Differentiating Content in an Inclusion Eleventh-Grade English Class

Planning Guide

Course: English III

Unit/Text: *The Color of Water* by James McBride

Poems: "Trying Hard to Be an American" by Pat Mora and "Theme in English B" by Langston Hughes

Essential Questions:
How do we define our own identity?
How does society judge people?
What does it mean to be an American?
How can a theme be represented in different genres?

Unit-Specific Questions:
How do the two poems connect to the novel *The Color of Water*?
Why would immigrants want to give up their cultural identity?

Knowledge/Skills:

Students will be able to:

- Understand the thematic connections among the novel and the two poems
- Understand the conflicts multiracial people and immigrants face in America historically and today

Modes of Differentiation Used:

Differentiate:

content: After reading the same novel, students read two different poems.

process: Students self-select the poem they wish to study, group studies.

Based on: interests

Strategies: student choice, small groups

English III Inclusion Class: Differentiating Content Using Groups

Louis is a special education student in an eleventh-grade English inclusion class that contains two co-teachers, an English teacher, Lauren O'Keefe, and a Special Education teacher, Kelly Maley, and a mix of classified and nonclassified students. Seven of the 20 students in the class are classified. Both teachers agreed that when forming partners and groups within the class, they would mix the students as much as possible and avoid creating a special education subclass. The two teachers planned many lessons that incorporate elements of differentiated instruction. During the summer, students are required to read James McBride's *The Color of Water*. This gives them a common text to study together the first few weeks of school. Lauren and Kelly decided to extend the unit to include two poems that are related thematically to the novel: "Trying Hard to Be an American" by Pat Mora and "Theme in English B" by Langston Hughes. The teachers considered assigning students to groups based on readiness because they initially judged one poem to be more challenging than the other, but they decided that the content of the poems was more important than the difficulty. Therefore, they allowed students to select the poem they wanted to study.

Louis, who generally does not like to read, is usually very quiet when the whole class is discussing a text, rarely volunteering his opinions. When his teachers offered the class a choice of two poems to study, Louis elected to join the group studying the Langston Hughes poem. After the students had made their choices, they divided into two groups, with each group moving to a side of the room to meet with one of the teachers. Louis was in Lauren O'Keefe's group. Lauren read the poem aloud once all the way through, and then she conducted a guided reading of the poem. Louis was one of the first to volunteer a response, saying," I never read anything like this before." Because the lesson allowed for differentiated content and small-group instruction, Louis was able to make a clear personal connection to a work of literature, something that rarely happened for him. In the discussion and written work that followed, it was clear that Louis understood the theme of the poem and how it related to the novel the class had read, and he was willing to discuss it with his classmates. Basing assignments on student interest is a powerful motivator.

Differentiating Assignments in a Basic Eleventh-Grade English Class

Planning Guide

Unit/Text: *The Taming of The Shrew* by William Shakespeare

Essential Questions:
What is universal about the relationships between men and women?
How does an author create humor?
How does humor convey truths about life?

Unit-Specific Questions:

How have relationships between men and women changed or not changed since Shakespeare's time?

How does Shakespeare use language to create humor?

Knowledge/Skills:

Students will be able to:

- Understand Shakespeare's language and how it creates humor
- Understand the relationships among the characters in the play

Modes of Differentiation Used:

Differentiate:

process: Students determine how much help they need.

product: Written products leveled based on student readiness.

Based on: readiness

Strategies: tiering assignment, individual conferences

Basic English III: Differentiating Process and Products

During a study of the first three acts of Shakespeare's *Taming of the Shrew*, Briana exhibited the ability to read and discuss the play on both a literal and an inferential level. Several of her classmates also demonstrated a more sophisticated understanding than other members of the class. For this reason, their teacher, April Gonzalez, decided to create a tiered assignment based on student readiness. Being a NASCAR fan, April labeled each tier with race car numbers rather than A, B, or C to draw attention away from ability levels (Figure 6.6). She assigned students to a "car" based on their understanding of the first three acts of the play. Each assignment has a different

Differentiated Instruction in the English Classroom

Figure 6–6

Ladies and Gentlemen . . . Start Your Engines!

Car #8

Directions: You must complete number 1, then choose either A or B.

1. In Act IV, scene i, Shakespeare uses wordplay to contribute to the humorous interchange between Grumio and Curtis, and to further develop character. Puns with the words "hot" and "cold," "tail" and "tale," "countenance," and "credit" are a few examples. Choose one of the puns and reread the passage. Explain how Shakespeare uses wordplay to add to the humor and to develop character. Be prepared to quote and to paraphrase some lines as you support your point.

A. By the end of Act IV, we have learned Petruchio's plan for taming Kate. He has starved her, kept her from sleep, and denied her nice things with the rationale that nothing is good enough for her. You are Kate, and you write a journal entry describing in detail how you are feeling and what you think about Petruchio and his actions.

B. By the end of Act IV, Petruchio shared his plan for taming Kate. He has starved her, kept her from sleep, and denied her nice things, saying that nothing is good enough for her. You are Petruchio, and you confide in your servant and friend Grumio. You explain why you treat Kate in this manner, using the excuse that nothing is good enough for her. You defend your reasoning by referring to some of Kate's actions toward you. Finally, you reveal your feelings about Kate and the marriage and what you plan to do next.

Ladies and Gentlemen . . . Start Your Engines!

Car #17

Directions: You must complete number 1, then choose either A or B.

1. Choose a 10-line passage from Act IV, scene iii, and paraphrase/modernize the language. Then explain how this passage relates to a theme in the play.

A. By the end of Act IV, we have learned Petruchio's plan for taming Kate. He has starved her, kept her from sleep, and denied her nice things, with the rationale that nothing is good enough for her. You are Kate, and you write a journal entry describing in detail how you are feeling and what you think about Petruchio and his actions.

Figure 6–6 *continued*

B. By the end of Act IV, Petruchio shared his plan for taming Kate. He has starved her, kept her from sleep, and denied her nice things, saying that nothing is good enough for her. You are Petruchio, and you confide in your servant and friend Grumio. You explain why you treat Kate in this manner, using the excuse that nothing is good enough for her. You defend your reasoning by referring to some of Kate's actions toward you. Finally, you reveal your feelings about Kate and the marriage and what you plan to do next.

Ladies and Gentlemen . . . Start Your Engines!

Car #24

Directions: You must complete number 1, then choose either A or B.

1. Reread pages 153–157. Describe how Hortensio feels about Bianca and explain why. Support your response with a direct quotation.

A. By the end of Act IV, we have learned Petruchio's plan for taming Kate. He has starved her, kept her from sleep, and denied her nice things, with the rationale that nothing is good enough for her. You are Kate, and you write a journal entry describing in detail how you are feeling and what you think about Petruchio and his actions.

B. By the end of Act IV, Petruchio shared his plan for taming Kate. He has starved her, kept her from sleep, and denied her nice things, saying that nothing is good enough for her. You are Petruchio, and you confide in your servant and friend Grumio. You explain why you treat Kate in this manner, using the excuse that nothing is good enough for her. You defend your reasoning by referring to some of Kate's actions toward you. Finally, you reveal your feelings about Kate and the marriage and what you plan to do next.

initial activity, followed by a common component that allows for student choice.

April told the class that they could begin the assignments in class but that they would be finishing most of the work at home. If students needed help, April instructed them to put their names on the board and said that she would confer with them individually in the order in which their names appeared. She also told them that they could work quietly with a partner if it would help them to begin the assignment. She believed this would allow the students to determine whether they needed differentiated instruction.

Briana was assigned to Car # 8. After reading the instructions for the first assignment, she put her name on the board and waited for April to call her to the conference table. While Briana was waiting to confer with the teacher, April suggested that she reread the section in the play where the puns occur. Briana reported that rereading helped. When she met with her teacher, she had a better idea of what kind of help she needed. April asked Briana what the stumbling block was, and Briana said she did not see what was so funny. This question led to a discussion between April and Briana of the many types of humor. Briana, like many young people, was used to more obvious or physical humor. After April talked Briana through one pun in the play, the student returned to her seat and began applying what she had just learned to another example.

By giving students the opportunity to confer individually with her, April was able to differentiate the type and amount of instruction students needed.

Differentiating Research in a College-Preparatory Eleventh-Grade English Class

Planning Guide

Course: Academic English III

Unit of Study/Text: *Their Eyes Were Watching God* by Zora Neale Hurston

Essential Questions:

How is a culture transmitted from one generation to the next?
How does the time and place in which an author lives affect the
works of literature he/she produces?

Unit-Specific Questions:
What role did the Harlem Renaissance play in the development
of American culture and literature?
Who were the main people in the Harlem Renaissance?

Knowledge/Skills:
Students will know:

- The history and people of the Harlem Renaissance
- The variety of arts represented by the Harlem Renaissance
- The life and works of Zora Neale Hurston

Students will be able to:

- Explain the influences of the Harlem Renaissance on American
  culture and literature
- Explain how the author's life is reflected in her writing

Modes of Differentiation Used

Differentiate:

content: Students are reading different material based on the
projects they select.

process: Students select the projects they wish to complete and
the number of points they wish to earn.

products: Students present their learning in different modes they
select.

Based on: readiness, interests, and learning styles

Strategies: student choice, outside reading of multiple texts, literature circles, oral reports

College Prep English III: Differentiating Research

Kyle, a student who is easily distracted, frequently appears not to take his work in English seriously. When his teacher, Zandrea Eagle, created an assignment on the Harlem Renaissance as an introduction to a unit on *Their Eyes Were Watching God* by Zora Neale Hurston, she did a prereading assessment of her students' knowledge of the Harlem Renaissance (Figure 6.7). She asked the students to share aloud one thing from the prereading list that they knew well enough to teach. Kyle spoke at length about the jazz music that came out of Harlem. She was surprised to discover that Kyle was one of the few students in class who knew the artists associated with this movement, especially the musicians.

Students frequently have difficulty connecting with this novel because they are unfamiliar with the author and time period in which she wrote. With this in mind, the teacher wanted to build background knowledge about the historical and cultural influences on Hurston. So when Zandrea presented the class with an assignment on this period (Figure 6.8), Kyle knew exactly which musician he was going to focus on: Duke Ellington. Zandrea noted that this was the first time in English class that Kyle appeared motivated to work on an assignment.

Kyle exemplifies what can happen in a classroom when teachers give students the chance to make personal connections and to investigate something they really care about. In addition to investigating the biography on Duke Ellington, Kyle compiled a compact disc of jazz music from the Harlem Renaissance and incorporated it into his oral presentation.

Figure 6–7

Name _____ Date _____

Prereading List for the Harlem Renaissance

Place a "T" next to the terms you know well enough to teach to someone else.

Place an "H" next to the terms you have heard of.

Place a question mark "?" next to terms that are new to you.

____ Harlem Renaissance	____ Langston Hughes
____ Zora Neale Hurston	____ jazz
____ Count Basie	____ Claude McKay
____ W. E. B. DuBois	____ Bessie Smith
____ Duke Ellington	____ James Weldon Johnson
____ Countee Cullen	____ author's voice

Write a sentence that includes one name or term you know from the list. Make certain that your sentence shows that you know the person or term. If you do not know any of the items, write one thoughtful question you have about the Harlem Renaissance.

Zandrea differentiated the projects based on student readiness, interests, and learning styles. By differentiating content and including student choice, this assignment gave students the opportunity to decide which areas they wanted to study and how many points they wanted to earn.

Figure 6–8

Harlem Renaissance Projects: Instructions to Students

Zora Neale Hurston, author of *Their Eyes Were Watching God*, is one of the more prominent figures of the Harlem Renaissance. During this time, many African-Americans moved to Harlem for a better way of life. This was a very prolific time for African-Americans in literature, visual, and performing arts. For your outside reading project, you are to select several of the assignments listed below. The grade you receive will be determined by how many points you can accrue for the assignments.

65 points or more	=	A
55–64 points	=	B
45–54 points	=	C
35–44 points	=	D
25–34 points	=	F

The assignments:

For up to 50 points: You are to write a process paper on the Harlem Renaissance. You are to research the beginnings of the Renaissance and the impact that it has had on American society, then and now. You are to focus on the literary, musical, and visual aspects of the movement. This is to be an overview of the Renaissance; try not to focus on one particular person. You will have to turn in note cards to show your progress. The rough draft of your paper will be due on January 7, 2003. The final draft will be due on January 15th.

For up to 40 points: Give an oral presentation on the Harlem Renaissance. Your presentation must be four to six minutes long, and you must have visuals. You are to research the beginnings of the Renaissance and the impact that it had on American society, then and now. You are to focus on the literary, musical, and visual aspects of the movement. This is to be an overview of the Renaissance; try not to focus on one particular person. You will have to turn in note cards to show your progress.

Figure 6–8 *continued*

For up to 30 points: You will write a biography on one of the following writers:

Jean Toomer	Marcus Garvey	Arthur Schomburg
Jessie Fauset	Angelina Grimke	Zora Neale Hurston
Alain Locke	James Weldon Johnson	W. E. B. DuBois
Claude McKay	Nella Larsen	
Countee Cullen	Anna Bontemps	

For up to 30 points: You will write a biography on one of the following jazz artists:

Billie Holiday	William Henry Webb	Count Basie
Bessie Smith	Duke Ellington	

For up to 20 points: You will read a short story and analyze it. Discuss setting, plot, climax, denouement (falling action), and characters. Choose a story written by one of the following authors:

Jean Toomer	Marcus Garvey	Arthur Schomburg
Jessie Fauset	Angelina Grimke	Zora Neale Hurston
Alain Locke	James Weldon Johnson	W. E. B. DuBois
Claude McKay	Nella Larsen	Langston Hughes
Countee Cullen	Anna Bontemp	

For up to 15 points: Read a poem and analyze it. Discuss voice. Choose from one of the following authors:

Gwendolyn Brooks	James Weldon Johnson
Countee Cullen	Claude McKay
Langston Hughes	Jean Toomer

For up to 15 points: Bring in artwork from the Harlem Renaissance with a brief explanation of the artifact.

For up to 10 points: Make an audiotape or CD of several musical artists from the jazz and blues era of the 1920s.

Differentiating Writing Assignments in a College Preparatory Twelfth-Grade English Class

Planning Guide

Course/Level: English IV Academic

Unit of Study/Text: *Things Fall Apart* by Chinua Achebe

Essential Questions:

Is there a universal morality or is it culturally defined?

How are a culture's values transmitted?

How are male and female roles defined in a culture?

How do authors represent the same theme in two different genres?

What are the attributes of a successful literary analysis paper?

Unit-Specific Questions:

How are the masculine and feminine roles represented in the novel?

What causes Okonkwo's fall?

How do different views of morality clash in the novel?

How are the novel and Yeats's poem "The Second Coming" related?

Skills

Students will know:

- The conflicts of colonialism in Africa, especially Nigeria
- The political, social, and moral issues presented in the novel

Students will be able to:

- Explain theme in the novel
- Explain the impact of colonialism on Africans
- Explain the connection between Yeats's poem and the novel

- Discuss the political, social, and moral issues presented in the novel
- Write a literary analysis paper

Modes of Differentiation Used:

Differentiate: products by offering tiered writing topics

Based on: readiness and interests

Strategies: tiered writing assignments and student choice, conferences

College Prep English IV: Differentiating Writing Assignments

When Andy Loh assigned an essay as the final activity in a unit on Chinua Achebe's *Things Fall Apart*, he began by introducing the writing rubric with which the essays would be assessed. Each student received a copy of the rubric, and Andy reviewed the criteria in class (see Figure 6.9). Andy wanted his students to be clear on the requirements of good essay writing before they began the assignment. The writing topics in the assignment (Figure 6.10) were tiered, representing different levels of difficulty. Based on the students' previous writing assignments and class discussions, Andy had an idea of which assignments he thought would be appropriate for each student, but he wanted to give these seniors a choice of topics. Therefore, he decided to confer with each student before he/she made a final selection.

When Leslie went to her conference with Andy, she had decided that she wanted to write about the moral issues in *Things Fall Apart* (number 3 shown on Figure 6.10). Leslie had been angered by some of the beliefs students presented during a class discussion of these issues. Andy had a different idea in mind before

Differentiated Instruction in the English Classroom

he met with Leslie. He knew that writing an essay that involved integrating different viewpoints was not easy for Leslie. She did better if the paper had one clear focus. During their conference, however, it became clear that Leslie had a strong commitment to the topic of how morality is defined. Her comments showed that she was a young woman with strong convictions. Andy then realized that his job would be to help Leslie organize her ideas.

After reviewing the rubric on writing with Leslie, Andy set up time to meet again after she had written a draft. Andy and Leslie met twice again. Andy noted that each time her paper became clearer and better organized. The one-on-one conferences gave Leslie and Andy the opportunity to concentrate on her unique writing problems. The teacher realized that when students feel strongly about a topic, they often can perform at a higher level than previously demonstrated. By differentiating the topics and offering the students a choice of writing topics that represented different degrees of challenge, Andy gave the students the freedom to stretch themselves academically. Leslie rose to the challenge and succeeded.

Differentiating Texts in a Tenth-Grade English Class

Planning Guide

Course: English II

Unit of Study/Text: American Short Stories

Essential Questions:
What are the literary elements that define a short story?
How do short stories differ from novels?
How do editors decide how to group short stories into collections?

Figure 6–9

	1	2	3	4
Textual Reference (8 points)	Little or no direct reference to text.	Some reference to the text but weak and/or sparse.	Much direct textual reference, but more is needed in order to prove thesis more strongly.	Essay refers directly to the text throughout and uses good, insightful examples to support the thesis.
Introduction (4 points)	Poor, lackluster or clichéd introduction; reader is not "hooked."	Attempt at an interesting introduction made, but it fails to "hook" the reader.	Introduction well thought out and refreshing, but there is still some room for improvement.	Introduction is innovative, catchy and tasteful; reader is "hooked."
Thesis Statement (4 points)	Weak/nonexistent thesis present.	Fair thesis present, but needs work to be viable.	Good thesis present, but could use a little more clarity.	Strong, clear thesis statement present.
Transitions (4 points)	Poor use of transitions; essay extremely choppy.	Attempt at transitions, but these are few or poorly orchestrated; much work still needed.	Transitions are used generously and well for the most part, but essay still does not flow as easily as it should.	Transitions are in place which contribute to a smooth, cohesive, easily read essay.
Organization/ Paragraph Structure (4 points)	Does not follow 5-paragraph structure.	Some attempts to follow 5-paragraph structure, but organization is not clear.	Follows 5-paragraph structure for the most part, but could still use better organization.	Well organized; follows 5-paragraph structure with Intro/Thesis, 3 Body Paragraphs and Conclusion.
Repetition and	Essay extremely	Some repetitions/	Minor repetitions or	No or few instances of

Category				
Redundancy (4 points)	repetitious and redundant to the point of distraction to the reader.	redundancies, that detract from cohesiveness of essay.	redundancies that do not detract from overall cohesiveness of essay.	repetitious words, phrases, or patterns.
G.U.M.S. and Revising* (4 points)	Extremely poor G.U.M.S. Needs much work.	Some patterns of errors that detract from the cohesiveness of the essay.	Some minor errors in G.U.M.S., but these do not really adversely affect the cohesiveness of the essay.	The essay has no or very few grammar and usage issues. There are few to no fragments, spelling errors, or poor mechanics/usage. Essay is very cohesive.
Conclusion (4 points)	Conclusion fails to "pull it all together" and leaves reader hanging.	Conclusion present but weak.	Conclusion is very good but still does not "pull it all together" quite as well as it could.	Conclusion "pulls it all together" and provides an excellent closing to the essay.
Present Tense in Literature (4 points)	Present tense not used in describing literature.	Attempts to use present tense, but needs a lot of work.	Present tense used fairly well with some minor lapses.	Present tense used correctly and thoroughly throughout the essay to describe the literature.
Overall Content (Does the essay answer the question?) (8 points)	Essay rambles; no consistency or clarity; off-topic; question unanswered.	Attempt at answering the question and at consistency/clarity, but needs major work.	Essay is well done, fairly consistent and clear for the most part; answers the question, but could still use additional work.	Essay answers the question in a clear, concise and well-thought-out-manner.

Created by Andy Loh

*G.U.M.S. = Grammar, Usage, Mechanics, Spelling, and Sentence Structure

Figure 6–10

Writing Assignment for *Things Fall Apart*

You will be writing an essay on Chinua Achebe's *Things Fall Apart*. Several topics are presented below. They are not presented in any particular order. After carefully reviewing the topics, you need to meet with me during conference time, and we will discuss which topic you would like to do. I will offer suggestions, but the ultimate choice of which topic you write about is yours. Please bring your copy of the scoring rubric to our meeting.

1. Explain the significance of the title, *Things Fall Apart*, by referring to both Achebe's novel and Yeats's poem, "The Second Coming."

2. The motif of masculinity vs. femininity is a central one in the novel. Explain how the struggle between masculinity and femininity contributes to Okonkwo's downfall.

3. This novel has led us to discuss cultural vs. universal morality. Is there such a thing as universal morality, or is all morality relative and subjective? If all morality is relative, how can human beings objectively determine right from wrong? If at least some morality is universal, how can human beings know when a moral code is universally binding? Use incidents from the novel to support your point of view.

4. It has been argued that Okonkwo falls because the culture does not support him. Agree or disagree with that statement. Use specifics from the novel to support your point of view.

Unit-Specific Questions:
How does a particular story adhere to the elements of short stories? How does a particular author use the literary elements to engage the reader?

Knowledge/Skills:
Students will know:

- The literary elements of a short story
- The plot structure of short stories

Students will be able to:

- Participate successfully in literature circles
- Explain the elements of a particular short story aloud to the whole class

Modes of Differentiation Used:

Differentiate:

content: Students are reading different material based on readiness.

process: Students participate in literature circles.

products: Students present their learning in different modes they select.

Based on: readiness and interests

Strategies: outside reading of multiple texts, literature circles, oral reports

English II: Differentiating Texts Using Literature Circles

Libby was not a reader. Allison would read all day. The challenge for their teacher was to find short stories that would hold Libby's attention yet not bore Allison. As Molly Oehrlein was planning a unit on the American Short Story, she had Libby and Allison and their classmates in mind. Molly found the stories in the textbook lacking because they did not represent enough of a range of difficulty. Molly's sophomore English class contained students who could do honors work and students who needed basic skills. She wanted short stories that would challenge all students yet would not be so difficult that some students would stop reading. Working with her colleagues and the school media specialist, Molly was able to identify short story collections for all readers. Because she wanted students to read different texts, Molly decided to use literature circles for this unit. The students would be reading the stories on their own outside of class and then meeting one day a week to discuss them in literature circles.

To form the groups for the literature circles, Molly combined student choice with her knowledge of the students' readiness. She developed a model for literature circles based on the work of Daniels (1994). She began by asking the students to write the names of three classmates they would like to work with. Knowing the students and knowing the range of texts that would be available to the groups, Molly then constructed the literature circles and decided that the students would work as a group to read six American short stories that were connected in some way. For example, the students could select stories that were written by women, minorities, or regional authors. They could choose to do a genre study of short stories, concentrating, for example, on science fiction, mystery, or adventure stories. Next, the whole class went to the media center, and the librarian presented a book talk on the collections of short stories available. After the book talk, students met in their groups and completed a planning sheet (Figure 6.11) on which they identified their "story unit," that is, what would connect the group of stories they selected.

Libby and four other students met and decided to read mysteries, something they had not had the opportunity to read in school before. Libby liked a mystery story she had read by Agatha Christie in eighth grade and thought she would enjoy these stories. Having traveled with her family in the West, Libby was attracted to a collection of short stories titled *The Mysterious West*. Edited by Tony Hillerman, all are set in the western United States from Alaska to New Mexico. Libby's group was ready to go. Before the groups could begin, their teacher had to review with the class the proce-

Figure 6–11

Group Planning Sheet   Members _____
Literature Circles   _____
Short Story Unit   _____

The title of our short story unit is _____

Three reasons this unit appeals to us:

1.

2.

3.

Possible short stories we would like to include in this unit are:

Title (use quotation marks)	Author	Source (underline)	Page #'s

dures for literature circles (Figures 6.12 and 6.13). Molly also reviewed with the class her discussion rubric for assessing participation in the group discussions (Figure 6.14). The students were then instructed to come to the next class ready to participate in the literature circles.

Libby's group decided to begin by reading "A Woman's Place" by D. R. Meredith. Her group agreed that Libby would be the word searcher for this first short-story discussion. During the first meeting of their literature circle, Libby's group wanted to jump right in and tell what they thought about the ending of the mystery, but the discussion leader reminded them that he had prepared questions to address. After the group had discussed these questions, it was Libby's turn to share vocabulary. Libby identified the following words for her group: complacency, bovine, formidable, superseded, and ad hoc. She had picked these words for two reasons: because they were new to her or because they were an integral part of the story. For example, "ad hoc" was new to her, and "formidable" was an important characteristic of the protagonist. When Libby presented her words to the group, she included the page numbers on which they could be found in the story. She then led the group in identifying the denotations and connotations of the words. As the other members of the group took turns presenting their tasks (literary investigator, world reporter, idea illustrator), Libby and her peers participated in discussions and took notes. Their teacher visited the group and reminded them to refer back to the unit's essential questions as they discussed the story.

The fact that their story was a mystery led to lively discussions concerning plot and who suspected what when. Libby commented that trying to guess the ending was "like a game." Having students select the stories and genre they wished to study worked well for this group. At the end of the first literary circle meeting, the

Differentiated Instruction in the English Classroom

Figure 6–12

Literature Circle Procedures

1. Literature Circles are designed to provide choice, encourage responsibility, foster collaboration, support diverse responses to text, and most of all, promote positive attitudes toward reading.

2. Lit Circles will meet approximately once every week.

3. At each meeting, your group will assign itself homework for the next week's meeting. All members will read the same text; in addition, you will have an individually assigned role to prepare.

4. When your group assigns roles for homework, ALWAYS have a Discussion Leader and a Word Detective. You should not do any one role more than THREE times.

5. During the Lit Circle meeting, each person will take turns sharing what he or she has prepared. Always begin with the Discussion Leader, and then your group can decide where to go from there. Your ultimate goal is to find out the answers to the Essential Questions for the unit.

6. When meeting, students should follow the individuals working with the partner or group and the group discussion rubrics.

7. You are responsible for taking notes during the Lit Circle discussions so that you are prepared to complete the Lit Log and Open-ended Response on your own. Both are due the following class.

8. If your group legitimately finishes its dicussion before the time allotted, you may work *individually* on your Lit Log or your Open-ended Response; however, if the teacher notices that the discussion is not thorough, the entire group is in jeopardy of losing credit.

9. As with any other assignment, if you miss class for any reason, you must find out what your group and individual assignments are so that you arrive prepared for class.

10. If you come to class unprepared, you will complete an alternative assignment during the time that your group meets.

Figure 6–13

Literature Circle Roles

Discussion Leader

Write down at least FIVE good discussion questions that you think your group would want to talk about based on the reading. Good questions would be open-ended kinds of questions such as ones that begin with words Why? . . . How? . . . If? . . . What if? . . . Your questions should come from ideas that you yourself had when reading on your own. In addition, the Discussion Director is also responsible for making sure your group stays on task and follows the Group Rubric at all times.

Word Detective

Identify at least FIVE especially important words in the assigned reading. Look for two types of words: words that are challenging or new to you and words that may be used in a new or interesting way. Be ready to tell the group why you picked each word. When your circle meets, you will help members find and discuss the denotations and connotations of these words, and you will look for thematic connections as well.

Literary Investigator

Search for at least FIVE special sections of the reading that the group should investigate. Choose passages that you find silly, suspenseful, unusual, well written, or meaningful. If the author uses literary devices that you think are particularly effective, your passage might contain figurative language, foreshadowing, symbolism, repetition, etc. When you meet, read each passage aloud, get your group members to respond, and then explain your own response.

Word Reporter

Find at least FIVE connections between the text and the world, and write down how and why you made the connection. In your circle, see whether others see similar connections. You might find connections to:

- Your own life or the life of someone you know
- Situations in your school or community
- Similar events in history
- Other works on the same theme or by the same author

Idea Illustrator

Draw anything about the story that you think is particularly interesting. Your drawing could be realistic, symbolic, or metaphorical. Do any kind of drawing or picture using any type of media that you like. When your group meets, do not tell what your artwork represents; let each member guess and talk about it first. Then you can explain what you intended when you created it.

Figure 6–14

Group Discussion Rubric

	ACCEPTABLE	UNACCEPTABLE
I D E A S	Being willing to participate by sharing ideas and information. Finding specific examples from your reading. Getting others to participate by encouraging and questioning them. Listening carefully; you may even change your own ideas. Stressing your own ideas and repeating if you have to.	Not sharing or participating at all. Saying things that aren't specific or that you can't prove. Dominating the discussion. Playing with items on desk, singing, whispering, writing notes, etc. Getting angry when others don't understand your ideas.
A T T I T U D E	Disagreeing with but respecting the speaker's views. Waiting patiently for your turn to speak; hearing others out. Treating the discussion maturely and seriously. Ignoring immature behavior or helping others not to be immature.	Laughing or rolling your eyes at the speaker. Shouting out or interrupting. Using sarcasm or bad language. Encouraging immature behavior by joining in or laughing at it.
P R E S E N C E	Speaking clearly and audibly. Having good eye contact with the speaker and audience. Having positive body language.	Mumbling or speaking too softly. Looking down, around the room, or only at the teacher. Slouching or putting your head down.

Developed by Molly Oehrlein and Erin Farrell

group discussion leader made certain that everyone agreed on the next story to read from the collection.

The examples presented in this chapter are lessons developed by teachers who are investigating ways to address the needs of all of their students. They used strategies that are already familiar to them, such as literature circles, and added new strategies such as learning stations. In each example, however, the teachers recognized that strategies alone do not constitute differentiated instruction. They began with identifying the strengths and needs of their students. Each time they teach a unit, these teachers establish the goals for that unit and then look at where their students are in relation to these goals.

Differentiated Instruction in the English Classroom

What Is the Relationship Between Differentiation of Instruction and Other Educational Beliefs and Practices?

Differentiation of instruction, as a way of thinking about teaching and learning, is akin to and supported by other educational beliefs or practices that place students at the center of instruction and view each student and his/her learning as uniquely individualistic. Gardner's (1983;1993) theory of multiple intelligences, which acknowledges different forms and ways of knowing—interpersonal/social, intrapersonal/introspective, mathematical/logical, verbal/linguistic, visual/spatial, musical/rhythmic, and bodily/kinesthetic, provides not only support for differentiation of instruction but also a formalized way to learn about students, their learning styles, and their subsequent ability to solve problems. Using Gardner's analytic and organic definition of intelligence can help a teacher to recognize and use objectives, learning experiences, and/or activities that will appeal to each student and allow each to be successful. Excellent resources exist for those who want and choose to differentiate instruction based solely or in part on Gardner's definition and theory. Fogarty and Stoehr's (1995) *Integrating Curricula with Multiple Intelligences*, in addition to containing much useful information about thematic instruction and teaming, offers a clear and concise two-page appendix derived from a training manual for curricula integration. This appendix, in chart form, details specific ways each intelligence experiences optimal learning and lists the types of activities that facilitate achievement for each type of intelligence. For example, those whose preference is the mathematical/logical intelligence learn optimally through collecting, recording, and ranking, using such activities as matrices, syllogisms, codes, and games. Lazear (1994), in *Multiple Intelligence Approaches to Assessment Solving the Assessment Conundrum*, provides a multiple intelligence assessment menu that can help teachers design activities and assessments that promote differentiated instruction. The ideas and suggestions from any of these resources can be effectively combined with the planning guide explained in this book. For example, the teacher, using this guide, can list under the section "Based on:" the specific intelligence targeted. Differentiation for content, process, or product can be tailored based on multiple intelligence theory, and this can be recorded under the guide's section: "Differentiate." This differentiation can be based on one's identified intelligence and can use strategies appropriate to this identified intelligence. For example, the differentiation example contained in Chapter 6, based on *Romeo and Juliet,* addresses both verbal/linguistic and interpersonal/social intelligences.

Another educational theory and practice that places students at the center of learning and instruction, constructivism, like differentiation of instruction, emphasizes the importance of the knowledge, beliefs, and skills an individual brings to the experi-

Differentiated Instruction in the English Classroom

ence of learning and recognizes the construction of new under-standing as a combination of prior learning, new information, and readiness to learn (Strickland and Strickland, 2002). Teachers who believe in constructivism also can see how the idea of differentia-tion of instruction supports their beliefs and furthermore can use differentiation strategies to meet student needs. Constructivist teaching presents students with problems to which they apply approaches they already know and integrate those approaches with alternatives presented by others, research sources, or current experience. Through trial and error, students blend preexisting views with new experiences to construct understanding. Teachers are facilitators, coaches, and co-learners. They challenge students to think critically and analyze throughout the learning experience. Specifically with regard to English teaching and learning, constructivist teachers are challenged to create classrooms that allow all students—regardless of linguistic and/or cultural back-ground to achieve at optimum levels. Using the methods and strat-egies of differentiation of instruction will help constructivist learners achieve at such levels. Differentiation of instruction, as explained by examples in this book, provides teaching strategies and methods that are practical alternatives to help teachers meet the needs of all in a heterogeneous classroom. Particularly, the ex-ample in Chapter 6, titled "Differentiating Content Using a Learn-ing Contract in Twelfth-Grade English," presents a way to help each student relate personally to the content. Justine's prior knowledge about the play is considered as she is challenged to construct a review based on feminist literary criticism.

Brain-based theories of instruction (Sousa 1995) are likewise compatible with differentiation of instruction. Differentiation, with its emphasis on providing activities so that individual learn-ers can link new knowledge with and through their levels of readi-ness, interests, and learning styles, supports brain-based learning theory in acknowledging that meaning making and learning are unique for each person. This uniqueness determines students' levels of readiness for new learning and is dependent on, among other things, long-term memory experiences and storage. Those who believe in brain-based research and who subsequently choose differentiation of instruction as a relevant and useful strategy will find *How the Brain Learns* (Sousa, 1995) helpful. This book provides specific teaching examples, besides detailing an easy-to-understand summary of recent brain-related research. Particularly relevant for differentiation tips and strategies is the discussion of teaching to both hemispheres (pp. 97–107). For example, Sousa suggests note taking, imagery, and concept mapping as various ways to teach learners to associate language with visual imagery. Additionally, Jensen (1998) suggests connecting to individual learners by asking them how they know what they know. He emphasizes that *how* questions ("How do you begin to read a poem?" "How does Harper Lee develop the character of Scout in *To Kill a Mockingbird*?" etc.) give teachers the opportunity to learn about each pupil's unique pattern and context of learning. Such learning about individual mental models provides the evidence for an instructor to begin to tailor teaching through differentiation. The example in Chapter 6, titled "Differentiating Content Using Stations in a Tenth-Grade English Class," demonstrates how learning stations can help students relate prior and new knowledge and offers a variety of teaching strategies as they study *The Crucible*.

The primarily elementary language arts concept and practice of balanced literacy instruction also is in accord with differentiation of instruction. Balanced literacy teaching involves providing learners with systematic instruction in the skills and strategies of reading, writing, speaking, and listening coupled with activities that are real and meaningful to the students. Like differentiation of instruction, it involves identifying and tapping into pupils' inter-

Differentiated Instruction in the English Classroom

ests and learning styles (Au, Carroll, and Scher, 1997). By definition, balanced literacy instruction necessitates the formation of a workshop approach that emphasizes individual progress and process as well as final outcomes. Various avenues, such as author studies, peer conferences, mini-lessons, book talks, and literature circles, help each learner to acquire the predetermined knowledge and skills. Many of the examples contained in Chapter 6 parallel balanced literacy practices. Particularly, the example titled "Differentiating Lessons Using Work Folders in a Skills-Based English Class" presents the workshop experience and validates the learner's—Lisa's—own experiences and viewpoint as her teacher asks her various questions.

Educational theories, philosophies, and practices such as multiple intelligence theory, constructivism, brain-based learning, and balanced literacy instruction, that place students at the center and acknowledge each learner as an individual are compatible with differentiation of instruction. All of these charge and challenge the teacher to find and adapt content, process, product, and assessment to fit the unique and diverse needs of each learner. Employing differentiation strategies and activities helps teachers answer this charge and challenge.

Works Cited

Adler, Mortimer. 1984. *The paideia proposal.* New York: Macmillan.

Atwell, Nancie. 1998. *In the middle.* 2d ed. Portsmouth, N.H.: Heinemann.

Au, Kathryn H., Jacquelin H. Carroll, and Judith A. Schev. 1997. *Balanced literacy instruction.* Norwood, Mass.: Christopher Gordon.

Ball, Wanda H., and Pam Brewer. 2000. *Socratic seminar in the block.* Larchmont, N.Y.: Eye on Education.

Bloom, Benjamin. 1956. *Taxonomy of educational objectives: Handbook I: Cognitive domain.* New York: McKay.

Burke, Jim. 1999. *An English teacher's companion.* Portsmouth, N.H.: Boynton/Cook.

———. 2000. *Reading reminders.* Portsmouth, N.H.: Heinemann.

Daniels, Harvey. 1994. *Literature circles: Voices and choices in the student centered classroom.* York, Maine: Stenhouse Publishers.

Dunn, Rita, and Kenneth Dunn. 1993. *Teaching secondary students through their individual learning styles.* Boston: Allyn and Bacon.

4-MAT coursebook, The, vol. I 1993. Boston: Allyn and Bacon.

Fogarty, Robin, and Judy Stoehr. 1995. *Integrating curricula with multiple intelligences.* Arlington Heights, Ill.: Skylight.

Gardner, Howard. 1983. *Frames of mind: The theory of multiple intelligences.* New York: Basic Books.

———. 1993. *Multiple intelligences: The theory in practice.* New York: HarperCollins.

Heacox, Diane. 2002. *Differentiating instruction in the regular classroom.* Minneapolis, Minn.: Free Spirit Publishing.

Hillerman, Tony, ed. 1994. *The mysterious west.* New York: Harper Collins.

Jensen, Eric. 1998. *Teaching with the brain in mind.* Alexandra, Va.: ASCD.

Kalil, Carolyn, John Lowry, and Mike Berry. 1999. *Follow your true colors to the work you love.* Concord, Ontario: Career Lifeskills Resources.

Keefe, James, W. and John M. Jenkins. 2002. "Personalized instruction." Phi Delta Kappan. 83 (6): 446–448.

Lazear, David. 1994. *Multiple intelligence approaches to assessment.* Tucson, Ariz.: Zephyr Press.

Macrorie, Ken. 1988. *The I-search paper: Revised edition of searching writing*. Portsmouth, N.H.: Heinemann.

Ogle, Donna. 1986. "K.W.L.: A teaching method that develops actual reading of expository text." *The reading teacher* 39: 563.

Owocki, Gretchen, and Yetta Goodman. 2002. *Kidwatching: documenting children's literacy development*. Portsmouth, N.H.: Heinemann.

Saphier, Jon and Robert Gower. 1997. *The skillful teacher: Building your teaching skills*. 5th ed. Carlisle, Mass.: Research for Better Teaching, Inc.

Sousa, David A. 1995. *How the brain learns*. Reston, Va.: National Association for Secondary Principals.

Strickland, Kathleen, and James Strickland. 2002. *Engaged in learning: Teaching English 6–12*. Portsmouth, N.H.: Heinemann.

Tomlinson, Carol Ann. September 1993. Independent study: A flexible tool for encouraging academic and personal growth. *Middle School Journal* 25:55.

———. 1999. *The differentiated classroom: Responding to the needs of all learners*. Alexandria, Va.: ASCD.

———. September 2000. Reconcilable differences? Standards-based teaching and differentiation. *Educational Leadership* 58 (1): 6–11.

———. 2001a. *How to differentiate instruction in mixed-ability classrooms*. Alexandria, Va.: ASCD.

———. 2001b Leadership for differentiated instruction. http://www.aasa.org/publications/sa/1999_10/tomlinson.html. November 26, 2001.

Wiggins, Grant, and Jamie McTighe. 1998. *Understanding by design*. Alexandria, Va.: ASCD.

Winebrenner, Susan. 2001. *Teaching gifted kids in the regular classroom*. Minneapolis, Minn.: Free Spirit Publishing Inc.

———. 2002b. Gifted Students Need an Education Too. *Educational Leadership* 58 (1): 52–56.

Wormeli, Rick. 2001. *Meet me in the middle*. Portland, Maine: Stenhouse.

Appendix A

Curriculum Compacting Agreement

Student's Name _____

Teacher's Name _____

Unit _____ Grade/Level _____

Knowledge/Skills Mastered _____

_____

_____

Evidence of Mastery _____

_____

Learning Plan _____

_____

_____

Resources Needed _____

_____

Product(s) to be submitted _____

_____

Completion Date _____

Student's Signature and Date _____

Teacher's Signature and Date _____

Appendix B

Independent Learning Contract

Student's Name _____

Teacher's Name _____

Topic/Text: _____

Reason for Contract: _____

Time frame: _____

Beginning Date: _____ Completion Date: _____

Independent Assignment: _____

_____

_____

Products: _____

_____

Assessment: _____

_____

_____

Student's Signature and Date _____

Teacher's Signature and Date _____

Index